Volume 1

SHAKESPEARE'S "HAMLET"

BOUND WITH

THE PROBLEM OF "HAMLET"

SHAKESPEARE'S "HAMLET"

A. CLUTTON-BROCK

BOUND WITH

THE PROBLEM OF "HAMLET"

J. M. ROBERTSON

Routledge
Taylor & Francis Group

LONDON AND NEW YORK

First published 2014 by Routledge

Shakespeare's "Hamlet" first published in 1922
The Problem of "Hamlet" first published in 1919

Published 2016 by Routledge

This edition published in 2014
by Routledge
2 Park Square, Milton Park, Abingdon, Oxon OX14 4RN

and by Routledge
711 Third Avenue, New York, NY 10017, USA

Routledge is an imprint of the Taylor & Francis Group, an informa business

First issued in paperback 2015

British Library Cataloguing in Publication Data
A catalogue record for this book is available from the British Library

ISBN 978-0-415-81961-9 (Set)
eISBN 978-1-315-81764-4 (Set)
ISBN 978-0-415-73279-6 (hbk) (Volume 1)
ISBN 978-1-138-99612-0 (pbk) (Volume 1)
ISBN 978-1-315-81769-9 (ebk) (Volume 1)

Publisher's Note
The publisher has gone to great lengths to ensure the quality of this book but points out that some imperfections from the original may be apparent.

Disclaimer
The publisher has made every effort to trace copyright holders and would welcome correspondence from those they have been unable to trace.

SHAKESPEARE'S "HAMLET"

BY

A. CLUTTON-BROCK

METHUEN & CO. LTD.
36 ESSEX STREET W.C.
LONDON

First Published in 1922

PREFACE

THE theory of *Hamlet*, which I state in the second chapter of this book, was first suggested to me by a performance of the play which Mr. William Poel gave some years before the war in the Little Theatre. It left out a good deal of the play and was imperfect in execution; but it seemed to me right in conception, and suddenly I understood Hamlet, or thought I did, and saw that it was not a puzzle but a masterpiece. I then tried to explain my understanding in an analysis of the play, but did not publish it because, I thought, enough and more than enough had been written about Hamlet. I am provoked to publish it now, after rewriting it, by the theories of Mr. J. M. Robertson and Mr. T. S. Eliot, with which I deal in my first chapter and which imply, or assert, that *Hamlet* is not a master-piece at all, but an accident or a failure. Mr. Eliot's criticism, in particular, seems to me to be based on a misunderstanding, not only of this play, but of the whole nature of art; and I am convinced by other criticism which I have read, that such misunderstanding is a common obstacle to the experience of art. I have therefore added a last chapter on *Hamlet* as an æsthetic document. I must make general acknowledgments to Mr. Bradley, whose essay on *Hamlet* I have mentioned once or twice; for it may be that I owe more to it than I know.

A. CLUTTON-BROCK

THE RED HOUSE, GODALMING
December 28, 1921

CONTENTS

SHAKESPEARE'S "HAMLET"

CHAPTER I

The Case against "Hamlet"

THOUGH *Hamlet* is the most acted, and discussed, of all Shakespeare's plays, perhaps of all plays that have ever been written, yet there is a case against it; and that case can best be stated in a question— What is the cause of Hamlet's delay in killing the King? It has been asked for two hundred years; in 1736 Hanmer, Mr. Bradley tells us, remarked that " there appears no reason at all in nature why this young Prince did not put the usurper to death as soon as possible"; and he continues, " If Shakespeare had made the young man go naturally to work, there would have been no play at all."[1] If this is so, then the case against *Hamlet* is proved; for a play, that can be prolonged only if the hero does

---

[1] The words quoted occur in an anonymous pamphlet. It is only conjecture that Sir Thomas Hanmer, an editor of Shakespeare, wrote them.

not go naturally to work, is bad in conception. But most of those who have discussed the delay have not accepted Hanmer's reason for it; they have found the cause either in Hamlet's circumstances or in his character; they say that he could not kill the King because he was so well guarded, or that he suffered from some mental impediment to the exercise of his will.

The first of these explanations would also condemn the play, if it were true; for it was Shakespeare's business to make us see that Hamlet was prevented by circumstances. But it is not true. The King, while praying, is exposed, unguarded, to Hamlet; and Hamlet himself says that he has means enough to kill him. His difficulty, whatever it may be, is not that. But, if the impediment is in his character, Shakespeare has still to meet the charge that he has not explained what that impediment is. He draws our attention to it, for Hamlet himself wonders why he does not kill the King; and writers, who have discussed the character of Hamlet, have given many reasons, some ingenious and some absurd but most of them subject to this objection, that they are guessed or imagined as if he were a real man, a person of history, instead of a character in a play. The difficulty of the problem lies in the fact that he is a character in a play and that therefore we must look for the causes of his behaviour in that play; we know nothing about him except what is in it, for there is nothing else to know. Why then has Shakespeare left the causes of his behaviour obscure to us, if he has left them obscure; why has he insisted that they were obscure to Hamlet himself?

Mr. J. M. Robertson has lately written a book, *The Problem of Hamlet*, in which he returns to Hanmer's answer, though he gives reasons for it which Hanmer did not give. The cause of the delay,[1] he says, is to be found, not in Hamlet's character nor in his circumstances, but in the circumstances of the play. Shakespeare, when he wrote *Hamlet*, was revising an old play, in which the young prince did not put the usurper to death as soon as possible, for the very reasons given by Hanmer. Shakespeare "simply decided to accept inexplicable delay as the formula of a play which

---

[1] Mr. Robertson also is inclined to deny even the fact of the delay; but that point I discuss in an Appendix.

reached him with that character apparently
stamped upon it." This old play does not
exist; but, as Mr Robertson says, it certainly
did exist in Shakespeare's time and was, very
likely, written by Thomas Kyd, the author of
The Spanish Tragedy—Mr. Robertson in-
geniously conjectures the character of this play
both from Kyd's other works and from a German
play, *Der Bestrafte Brodermord*, which may
have been a version of it. The German play,
which I have not read, appears from Mr.
Robertson's account of it to be a crude drama
of revenge delayed by expedients; and, as Mr.
Robertson says, we should expect from Kyd a
" delayed revenge as in the *Tragedy*, but a revenge delayed simply—or partly—through lack
of opportunity or fear of miscarriage, as in that
case," though this would not be " inexplicable
delay." Certainly we should not expect a
play, or a character, at all like Shakespeare's
Hamlet. It will be seen, therefore, that, since
we know nothing of Kyd's play, the extent of
its influence upon *Hamlet* must be conjecture;
and further that, if indeed the delay in *Hamlet*
is simply an inheritance from Kyd for which
Shakespeare fails to account, then *Hamlet* is

not the masterpiece it has always been called, and the problem is not one of Hamlet's conduct but of Shakespeare's misconduct.

Mr. Robertson conjectures that Kyd did account for the delay in some crude, mechanical, way, such as lack of opportunity, or fear of miscarriage, but that Shakespeare, for reasons which are difficult to understand, left out Kyd's explanation without providing one of his own; in fact left Hamlet himself wondering why he did not kill the King, and has left us all wondering ever since with good reason, since the cause was to be found, not in *Hamlet* at all, but in the lost work of Kyd.

If this is true, the proof of it is to be found only in *Hamlet*; and Mr. Robertson tries to find it there. But a great part of his ingenious attempt is irrelevant, since it is not concerned with the delay, but with other matters. He believes, for instance, that Kyd's play was in two parts and that *Hamlet* is so long because Shakespeare crowded the two parts into one; but that has nothing to do with the problem of the delay, unless we suppose that Shakespeare was forced to crowd out all Kyd's explanations of that delay; in which case he was merely incompetent. Then, he says, there are irrelevant scenes in *Hamlet* which survive from Kyd; but these, if they exist, also have nothing to do with the problem of the delay; and why did Shakespeare retain them if he was forced to crowd out Kyd's explanations? One of them is the scene between Reynaldo and Polonius, which Mr. Robertson calls purposeless. But, not only does it come immediately after the great scene between Hamlet and the Ghost, to which it is a relief; it also leads into the first scene between Polonius and Ophelia; and it exhibits Polonius fussing about both of his children. We have no right to suspect it unless it is irrelevant beyond Shakespeare's usage, which it is not.[1] But Mr. Robertson is in a difficulty with this scene since there is nothing in it that suggests Kyd's method, let alone his style. He therefore conjectures that it was inserted by Chapman (and perhaps revised by Shakespeare) because " such irrelevant scene-writing is the speciality of Chapman." But he has begun by supposing that the scene is

[1] In *Hamlet* itself the passage about the child-actors is much more irrelevant but is certainly Shakespeare's, since it refers to events later than the possible date of the old play.

irrelevant in Hamlet because it is a survival from Kyd's play, in which there is no reason to suppose it was irrelevant. He is here torn between his desire to prove the influence of Kyd by the survival of matter irrelevant to Shakespeare's play, and his theory that Chapman was a kind of "affable, familiar ghost" who went about inserting irrelevant scenes in other men's plays. But he can't have it both ways. If the irrelevance of the scene is a proof that it survives from Kyd's play, it cannot be a product of Chapman's passion for irrelevance. Chapman may just as well have played his tricks on Shakespeare as on Kyd.

Mr. Robertson also speculates about the Fortinbras episodes; but these, whether or no they are irrelevant, have nothing to do with the problem of Hamlet's delay. They are, he says, "in no way necessary, as the play stands, to the final action; and, for that very reason, to suppose that Shakespeare invented them is to impute to him a kind of gratuitous mis-management impossible to him as a practical playwright. Rather we must assume that they too were given him; and pronounce that his error lay in retaining them." This is a curious argument coming from Mr. Robertson, who imputes to Shakespeare a gratuitous mismanagement much greater. A few superfluous scenes in an Elizabethan play matter little, if they are short; for the Elizabethan method, and particularly Shakespeare's, is a swift succession of scenes changing easily from one into another. There is no pretence of giving a whole story but rather a search-light seems to be thrown here and there upon a moving stream of events; it is a method which must be understood if we are to understand Shakespeare's stage-craft or the manner in which his plays should be acted. But it does matter much, in Elizabethan as in any drama, if, in the revision of a play, the delay in the main action is retained but the causes of it are not. That would indeed be gratuitous mismanagement, impossible to Shakespeare or indeed to anyone. I am not concerned to deny that the Fortinbras episodes may have been retained from the earlier play; but the fact that they are usually cut out of modern performances does not prove them irrelevant; modern performances usually reconstruct *Hamlet* into a different kind of play, losing the swift succession of scenes and the search-light effect for the sake of scenery and spectacle. One would need to see *Hamlet* performed as Shakespeare meant it to be performed, before one could judge what, if anything, was irrelevant in it. But, even if everything is irrelevant which Mr. Robertson calls so, that would only go to prove that Shakespeare did rewrite an old play, which is not denied ; it would not prove that, from mere carelessness or incompetence, he decided to accept inexplicable delay as the formula of the play, especially if, in the old play, the delay was, however mechanically, explained.

But Mr. Robertson seems to think that Shakespeare was, in some way, *compelled* thus to retain the formula of delay, while dropping the reasons for it. " It is easy to show that, while Shakespeare is certainly capable of oversight and of occasional confusion, in this case he has suffered or accepted compulsion imposed by material which, as a stage manager revising a popular play of marked action, he did not care to reject." What was this compulsion? If there was any compulsion at all, it must have been given a certain plot, to retain the

dramatic essence of that plot and not to retain
certain scenes and episodes which, according to
Mr. Robertson, are clearly superfluous. There
was nothing to prevent Shakespeare from cutting out the Fortinbras and the Reynaldo
episodes; there was everything to prevent him
from cutting out the very mainspring of the
plot, without finding another to put in its
place. Mr. Robertson does not suggest that
Shakespeare was in a hurry; he admits that
" In *Hamlet*, the first of the great plays in
which Shakespeare fully reveals his supremacy,
there is far more evidence of superabundant
power, and of keen interest in the main theme
than of haste or carelessness." Therefore, if
Shakespeare did ignore Kyd's causes for the
delay, he must have had his reasons for doing
so; it was not a matter of compulsion at all.
Shakespeare, when he wrote *Hamlet*, was no
longer the mere " factotum " that Green called
him about ten years before; he was, perhaps,
the most successful playwright of his time. If
he chose to rewrite an old play, he could make
what he would of it; he did rewrite the whole
of *Hamlet*, and, on Mr. Robertson's own show-
ing, so freely that he left out an essential part of

Kyd's play. What then becomes of the notion that, while leaving it out, he was " compelled " to put nothing else in to take its place?

(There is evidence, perhaps, that Shakespeare took more pains with *Hamlet* than with any other play, in the fact that there exists an earlier version of it, the Quarto of 1603. I am not concerned here to discuss the difficult problem of that earlier version, which seems to consist partly of Shakespeare's work garbled and partly of fragments of the older play, because there is much uncertainty about the manner in which it came into being. There is, at any rate, no reason to suppose that it gives us a version of the play which was at any time Shakespeare's own version. It seems rather a hotch-potch of Shakespeare and the older play, put together perhaps by some one who got Shakespeare's part of it furtively as well as imperfectly. Our document for Shakespeare's intentions and procedure is only *Hamlet* in its final versions; and this, I think, Mr. Robertson himself would allow. I therefore ignore the 1603 Quarto, except to say that, if it proves anything at all about Shakespeare's *Hamlet*, which I doubt, it proves only that he made an earlier version which he afterwards revised, and therefore that he took unusual pains with it.)

Mr. Robertson insists in the passage I have quoted from him that Kyd's *Hamlet* was a play of marked action. His theory seems to be that Shakespeare was compelled to retain that marked action as being the essence of the play; he means, I suppose, that the audience would have resented the absence of incidents to which they were accustomed; they would have said it was *Hamlet*, not without the Prince of Denmark, but without the ghost, the madness, the sudden deaths; it was not Hamlet himself that interested them but these things. Shakespeare, however, whatever compulsion he was subject to, was interested in Hamlet himself; and he has succeeded so well in communicating his interest to us that "*Hamlet* without the Prince of Denmark" means something with the point left out. We may assume that for Shakespeare, as for us, the character of Hamlet was the thing. In spite of all the compulsion put on him, he did try to transform the play from one of incident into one of character; and Mr. Robertson admits that he succeeded, although he was forced to exhibit that character through a series of incidents for which there remains no adequate cause. Mr. Robertson, indeed, praises the play as much as he blames it, and even more. Kyd, he says, had complicated a crude and simple old story with delays which he explained mechanically and not psychologically; " Shakespeare by immensely heightening the character (of Hamlet) puts it into still further irrelation with the action, giving us one great satisfaction in forgoing another." But could we be satisfied with a play in which the hero, more predominant perhaps than any hero in any other play whatever, was out of relation with the action, and that action of extreme violence ? Mr. Robertson seems to think we could, because, in fact, the world has been satisfied with *Hamlet* as a play, in spite of his theory about it. Shakespeare's triumph was, he says, " to turn a crude play into the masterpiece which he has left us. It is a perfectly magnificent *tour de force*, and its ultimate æsthetic miscarriage is only the supreme illustration of the vulgar but ancient truth that an entirely satisfactory silken purse cannot be constructed, even by a Shakespeare, out of a sow's ear."

But Mr. Robertson is a very honest as well as a learned writer, and, whatever we may think of his case, we cannot complain of the manner in which he presents it. He states his evidence accurately, and, what is more difficult, states fairly the deductions he draws from it. He does not deny the merits of *Hamlet* and is, indeed, hampered throughout by his acknowledgment of them. Though I think him mistaken, I have learned much from his book; and his examination of the current theories about Hamlet's character is both just and amusing.

Another critic who has lately attacked Hamlet, does not share his scruples or make his admissions. Mr. T. S. Eliot's " Hamlet and his Problems," published in his volume of essays, *The Sacred Wood*, is based on Mr. Robertson's book, but he comes to the conclusion, rather, I suspect, from reading that book than from reading *Hamlet*, that the play, " so far from being Shakespeare's masterpiece, is most certainly an artistic failure." " Probably," he thinks, " more people have found *Hamlet* a work of art because they have found it interesting, than have found it interesting because they have found it a work of art." That is, indeed, the natural process; but Mr. Eliot reverses it on principle and finds that *Coriolanus* is a greater play than *Hamlet*. He does not quite dare to say that he finds it more interesting; and, if he did, it would be difficult to believe him.

Mr. Eliot qualifies the word *failure* by the word *artistic*, no doubt because he remembers that for three centuries *Hamlet* has been, in every other respect, the most successful play that ever was written. That may be the reason why he is resolved to find it an artistic failure; for his arguments raise the suspicion that his conclusion is based, not on them, but on some strong, unconscious wish to reach that conclusion. These arguments are partly taken from Mr. Robertson, though not stated with his accuracy, and partly Mr. Eliot's own. Of the manner in which he uses Mr. Robertson's arguments, I will give two examples.

He contends that *Hamlet* " is superposed upon much cruder material which persists even in the final form "; and, in proof of that contention, he says that there are in the final version of *Hamlet* " verbal parallels so close to *The Spanish Tragedy* as to leave no doubt that in places Shakespeare was merely *revising* the text of Kyd." What are these parallels which prove revision? Mr. Robertson gives several parallels between Kyd and *Hamlet* but most of them are between Kyd and the Quarto of 1603. He says himself of the two most important that they disappear in the Second Quarto and the Folio, and that they are plainly Kyd's. One of them indeed is in a speech of the Queen's where she agrees to help Hamlet against the King. It does not belong to Shakespeare's conception of the play at all and is a proof of his departure from the older play, not of his compulsion to follow it. I would ask the reader to remember that no one denies the existence of an older play, or that Shakespeare did, in some respects, follow it, or that traces and fragments of this older play are to be found in the 1603 Quarto. But Mr. Eliot's contention goes much further than that; it is that *Hamlet* is an artistic failure because Shakespeare was revising a play of Kyd's and

The Case against " Hamlet "

that the cruder material persists in his final
form. Where are the parallels in the final
version of *Hamlet* which prove this? Mr.
Robertson does give some parallels between
Kyd and the final *Hamlet* and I will give
them too, so that the reader may test Mr.
Eliot's assertion for himself—

Kyd, in *The Spanish Tragedy* has—

> " And if the world like not this Tragedy,
>   Hard is the hap of old Hieronimo."

Hamlet (Act III. Scene II.) says—

> " For if the King like not the comedy,
>   Why then, belike,—he likes it not, perdy."

Here I wonder that Mr. Robertson, at
least, has not seen that Shakespeare was
actually quoting, and misquoting, Kyd, and
meaning the audience to see it. Just before,
Hamlet has quoted two stanzas, probably
from old ballads, and has clearly misquoted
the last line of the second stanza—" A very,
very — pajock "; after which Horatio says
" You might have rhymed." So Hamlet
reverses the process of misquotation and
rhymes where Kyd had not rhymed. Mr.
Robertson notes that the Quarto of 1603

reads—" For if the King like not the *Tragedy*,"
following Kyd more closely. We may conjecture that some one here, whether the printer
or the procurer of the version, recognized the
quotation from Kyd and thought that *Comedy*
was a mistake for *Tragedy*, or else did not
notice Shakespeare's difference. The suggestion
that Shakespeare was here retaining a line of
Kyd's (which Kyd himself must have copied
from another play of his own) because he
would not be at the pains to write his own play,
and that in a scene of the greatest moment
where he is at the height of his powers, is
—well, I do not think it needs discussing.

As for the other parallels—there are two,
taken, not from *The Spanish Tragedy* but
from *Soliman and Perseda*—

Kyd.	" Fair locks resembling Phœbus' radiant beams, Smooth forehead like the table of high Jove."
Shakespeare.	" Hyperion's curls ; the front of Jove himself."

and

Kyd.	" Importing health and wealth of Soliman.
Shakespeare.	" Importing Denmark's health and England's too."

These do not seem to me to be parallels at all; but I give them because Mr. Robertson gives them, noting that in the first there are no verbal identities except the word *Jove*—and Mr. Eliot speaks of verbal parallels—and that in the second only the unremarkable words *health* and *importing* are the same. If Shakespeare did remember these from *Soliman and Perseda*, he may well have done so unconsciously; there is no proof, and no reason to believe, that he was retaining them from Kyd.

These, so far as I know, are the only alleged parallels between Kyd and the final version of Hamlet; at least Mr. Robertson gives no others, and he is usually to be trusted to do all that can be done in the way of parallels, and even a little more. Mr. Eliot himself gives none at all, but only asserts that they exist and are so close as to leave no doubt that Shakespeare was in places revising the text of Kyd. By such methods I could prove, I think, that *Paradise Lost* was a revision of the text of a (lost) poem by Sylvester, or indeed by any poet who wrote before Milton.

Mr. Eliot's next argument for a revised text is stranger but not stronger. Still following, or seeming to follow, Mr. Robertson, he says that "finally there are unexplained scenes— the Polonius-Laertes, and the Polonius-Reynaldo scenes—for which there is little excuse ; these scenes are not in the verse style of Kyd, and not beyond doubt in the style of Shakespeare." I have already dealt with the Reynaldo scene ; and Mr. Robertson does not speak of the Polonius-Laertes scene at all, for the very good reason that there is no such scene in *Hamlet*. There is, of course, the famous speech of Polonius in which he gives advice to Laertes ; but how Mr. Eliot comes to speak of it as the Polonius-Laertes scene, or to couple it with the Reynaldo scene as unexplained or without excuse, I do not understand. It consists of 31 lines and comes in the middle of a scene, first between Laertes and Ophelia, and then between Polonius and Ophelia, which contains 135 lines and is entirely relevant to the play. Mr. Eliot, I take it, does not condemn the whole scene ; for, if he did, he might as well condemn the whole play as being by Kyd with irrelevances supplied, like the "lyrics" in a musical comedy, by Chapman. Therefore

what he condemns is the speech of Polonius,
which, for the purposes of his argument, he
calls the Polonius-Laertes scene; and this
speech, though not in the style of Kyd and
probably inserted by Chapman in his passion
for irrelevance, is for him a proof that
Shakespeare was merely revising the text of
Kyd.

But he has also psychological arguments to
which I will give some attention, because they
are of a kind very common in modern criticism
and because they involve a common æsthetic
fallacy. They are inconsistent with his other
arguments because they imply that Shakespeare
was not merely revising a play by Kyd.
"Shakespeare's *Hamlet*," he says, "so far as
it is Shakespeare's, is a play dealing with
the effect of a mother's guilt upon her son,
and Shakespeare was unable to impose this
motive successfully upon the intractable
material of the old play." Here, to begin
with, is the commonest of all critical errors.
The motive of the play is discovered
and defined — it is the effect of a mother's
guilt upon her son — and then we are
told that the play is a failure because that

motive will not explain everything in the play. But you have no right thus to discover motives in a play as if it were a history of real persons. Certainly the effect of Gertrude's guilt upon Hamlet is part of the play, but only so much as appears in the play itself. Because Mr. Eliot thinks it ought to dominate everything, while, in fact, it does not dominate everything, he says that Shakespeare was unable to impose this motive on the intractable material of the old play. But he thinks that Shakespeare was also trying to express in *Hamlet* something he could not express. "*Hamlet*, like the sonnets, is full of some stuff that the writer could not drag to light, contemplate, or manipulate into art." How does Mr. Eliot know this? " Hamlet, the man," he says, " is dominated by an emotion which is inexpressible, because it is in excess of the facts as they appear." Here I would ask the reader to remember the facts. Hamlet has learned, and from his father's Ghost, that that father has been murdered by his brother ; and further that his father's wife, and his own mother, has been the paramour of the murderer, whom she married within two months of the murder. Could any emotion be in excess of these facts? But Mr. Eliot then puts his case another way. Hamlet, he says, is baffled " by the absence of objective equivalent to his feelings "; which no doubt is true, and which means, not that his emotion is in excess of the facts, but that it is, naturally, so great that he cannot express it in any normal speech or action. Consequently he does not express it as Mr. Eliot, and others, would expect him to express it. That being so, Mr. Eliot concludes that his bafflement is " a prolongation of the bafflement of his creator in the face of his artistic problem." But Shakespeare's artistic problem was to make Hamlet behave as he would behave in those circumstances, and out of his behaviour to make a play. The question is whether or no he has done this, not whether Mr. Eliot, or anyone else, is unable to explain his behaviour in psychological terms.

The play would be an artistic failure if, seeing it acted on the stage, we found ourselves asking—" Why does Hamlet behave thus? " or protesting—" But he would not behave thus." No one, I think, has ever made that protest. Mr. Eliot himself does not make it; and, as for the question, it is asked often enough, but not, I think, during our actual æsthetic experience of the play. That is to say, it is not an æsthetic problem at all but an intellectual, a psychological, problem, such as might arise about the behaviour of anyone in real life; and it arises just because Hamlet convinces us so utterly while we are æsthetically experiencing the play.

But Mr. Eliot takes this intellectual for an æsthetic problem. Because "none of the possible actions can satisfy Hamlet" therefore "nothing that Shakespeare can do with the plot can express Hamlet for him"; and the conclusion is—" We must simply admit that here Shakespeare tackled a problem which proved too much for him." Again, because there is an intellectual problem which proves too much for Mr. Eliot, he concludes that the æsthetic problem has proved too much for Shakespeare. But was any character in drama ever *expressed* more completely than Hamlet? He may not be *explained*, to Mr. Eliot's satisfaction; but that was not Shakespeare's task. It is the essence of the tragedy that none of the possible actions can satisfy Hamlet, and for reasons which I shall try to explain in my second chapter; but, though Hamlet's behaviour may seem to us unintelligible psychologically, we are, æsthetically, convinced by it. As he acts, we feel, so he would act; and that is all we have a right to demand of the dramatist. There is no play that gives us a stronger feeling of certainty, and this must come from Shakespeare himself. He knew what Hamlet would do, though he did not know why he would do it; he saw Hamlet actually doing it, saw him speaking, thinking, feeling and acting, as if he were a real man; and so makes him real to us. Mr. Eliot says in an essay on Massinger, what he should have remembered in his essay on Hamlet, that " what the creator of a character needs is not so much knowledge of motives as keen sensibility; the dramatist need not understand people but he must be exceptionally aware of them." Shakespeare, I think, was more aware of Hamlet than of any other of his characters; he even gives to Hamlet a peculiar style of his own, a way of speaking which is his and no one else's, both in verse and in prose, and this awareness is what makes the play so interesting to us. Shakespeare himself was in love with the character and puts us in love with him, though he does many things which trouble us. In fact the tragedy lies in this, that he does so many things which trouble us, which seem contrary to his real character; and yet we never doubt that he would do them.

Mr. Eliot, when he says that Shakespeare, like Hamlet himself, was baffled by his problem, seems to imply that Hamlet can do nothing; but, in fact he does many things, though they may not be what we expect him to do. If *Hamlet* were a play in which nothing happened but talk, and if all the talk without action wearied us, then Mr. Eliot would be right; but *Hamlet* is exciting as a bloody melodrama to those who see nothing else in it. So far from spoiling an old play by leaving out the point of it, Shakespeare, we cannot doubt, has surpassed it in that very excitement which was Kyd's strong point. Yet, with all this action, he is all the while discovering the character of Hamlet to us, not in spite of the action but through it. The more I consider the facts, the more I wonder what, when Mr. Eliot says that the play is most certainly an artistic failure, he means by the word *artistic*.

He can only mean *scientific*; and, in fact, he condemns *Hamlet* because its success is so purely artistic, and prefers *Coriolanus* because it is far less purely a work of art. You can detach from *Coriolanus* a concept, a moral even; and you can therefore feel that the play is well wrought to illustrate this concept or this moral. You can say that a certain situation of universal interest is presented in it; and of this situation you can think apart from the play. But you cannot find any concept, any moral, any situation of universal interest in *Hamlet*, which can be detached from the play or thought of apart from it. The difference is this, that *Coriolanus* is made for its theme whereas *Hamlet* *is* its theme; and Mr. Eliot, like many other critics, prefers the former because it gives him something about which he can come to intellectual conclusions; whereas the latter only gives him a human being so vivid and moving that thought is baffled by him. *Coriolanus* is a descriptive play compared with *Hamlet*, which is creative; in *Coriolanus* we are aware of events more than of people, and the people seem to be there to illustrate the events. But in *Hamlet* we are aware of Hamlet himself more than of any events—the events interest us because they happen to him—and it is only when he is no longer before us that we begin to discuss the events and their causes. I say— we are aware of Hamlet—because the pre- dominance of the hero is a peculiarity, not a defect, of this play. The other characters are all living but, compared with him, they are slight; and they all seem to be there because of some point at which they contrast with him. In *Othello* Iago is a protagonist as well as Othello. In *King Lear* Cordelia, Goneril, the Fool and Edmund are remembered as clearly as Lear himself; in *Macbeth* there is also Lady Macbeth. But in *Hamlet* there is no one to compare with Hamlet; yet the play seems as fully populated as any other, for he fills it even when he is not on the stage.

So it is a great play and, as a work of art, a triumphant success in spite of the questions of all the critics. The business of drama is character and action, not psychology, which is science, not art. But action does not be- come action until performed by people who are real to us; and, as the reality of the people is manifested in action, so the reality of the action depends on that of the people. You may, if you will, psychologize about Hamlet—I shall do so myself in the next chapter—you may seek for the cause of his actions within his mind; but you do so because they are to you the actions of a real man; and the fact that you may not see why he does them does not make them less real or less dramatic.

Othello is usually supposed to have been the next of the great tragedies composed after *Hamlet*; the same objection might be made to Iago that Mr. Eliot makes to Hamlet, and far more justly. His emotion does indeed seem to be in excess of the facts as they appear; yet he convinces us, although we may not be able to explain the connexion between his emotion and his action in psychological terms. Shakespeare himself seems to have been aware of this difficulty and, in this case, to have feared that the audience would be puzzled by it, would ask questions which he did not wish them to ask and which he could not answer in the play; for he makes Iago give reasons for his conduct which are certainly

not the true ones and which differ from time
to time. These reasons, which are expressed
in melodramatic terms, must have been meant
for those of his audience who, like Mr. Eliot,
were not content with the reality of a character
but wanted to know why he did things. We
may guess that Shakespeare had met a man
like Iago—he has the air of being drawn from
life—and had realized him completely; it was
enough for him that he knew how Iago would
behave in given circumstances, and, if he gave
reasons for his behaviour, it was merely to
remove from the minds of his audience obstructions to their æsthetic experience.

There is a hint of the same kind of false,
but convenient, explanation in *Hamlet* also;
for, after his interview with the Ghost, Hamlet
says he may hereafter think fit to put an antic
disposition on. It is not what the real Hamlet
would say, but Shakespeare put it in to prevent
questions, which it would do all the more
surely because in the old play Hamlet had
probably feigned madness to avert the suspicions
of the King. Shakespeare does not give this
reason, which would have been going too far in
falsehood, since, in his play, the suspicions of

the King are aroused, rather than allayed, by Hamlet's antic disposition.

It may be thought that I have been too laborious in defending *Hamlet* against these attacks upon it; but the notions implied in them, that works of art are to be understood only through their history, and that they ought to answer questions which belong to science, are common obstructions to the experience of art. They need refuting, and can be better refuted in particular examples than in general terms. But there still remains the question—" Why did Hamlet delay to kill the King?"; and to that I wish to find an answer, so that it may no longer be an obstacle to anyone's experience of the play. Further, I believe that, the more fully we experience the play, the more we shall see that the delay, given the circumstances and Hamlet's character, is inevitable. During that experience we are not interested in the delay—indeed we hardly notice it—for, as in all the greatest dramas, what interests us is what is happening, not why it happens, or what is going to happen. We are absorbed by Hamlet himself and all that he says and does, which has the necessary sequence of notes in a great piece of music. But still, I think, the delay may be explained in psychological terms; and a psychological understanding of it may even heighten our experience of the play. At any rate it will remove an æsthetic irrelevance; and that, though a humble task, is worth doing.

CHAPTER II

Why Hamlet delayed to kill the King ✆

I WILL begin my explanation of the delay
by laying down the principle that nothing
which may be said about any character in
a play is of any value unless it can be expressed by that character on the stage, or, at
least, unless it is an assistance to the acting
of that character; for characters in a play
have no existence except in their parts, as
figures in a picture have no existence except
in the picture. But there is this difference
between a play and a picture, that a play
exists fully only when it is acted; it is like
music and needs executants. So in a play
there is more than the words, although often
we can deduce that more only from the words.
That is so in the case of *Hamlet.* We cannot
doubt that to Shakespeare and his company
the play was more than the words; he, being

a master of the stage, not only wrote the play but saw it being acted as he wrote it, and the words were only a part of it for him. They were communicated to the players in writing, but the rest of the play, the business, was communicated to them orally by Shakespeare himself; and this business was as much a part of the play as the words. Further, it is possible that all the business was not devised by Shakespeare; an executant may also be a creator and Burbage may have helped to create *Hamlet* in its fullest and most authentic life. He may here and there have seen more in his part than Shakespeare himself had seen; and Shakespeare may have joyfully consented to his discoveries.

So it is the business of an actor always, since a play lives fully only on the stage, to make what discoveries he can about his part. And this he must do, when all tradition of the original business is lost, out of the words alone. The test of his discoveries is, whether they can be acted, and whether they fit the part as the dramatist has written it. If they do, they may actually elucidate some obscurity in the words, may be a rediscovery of some business with which the playwright himself explained the meaning of his words. But it is not only an actor who can make such discoveries or rediscoveries. It is open to anyone to say how he thinks a play or a part ought to be acted; for, in saying this, he gives his opinion of the real and full meaning of the play. He is not passing away from the play, or the character, into psychology or into an imagined history of the character as he was when off the stage. He is not, for instance, telling what Hamlet learned at Wittenburg; he is merely deducing the rest of the part from the words. But, if he goes beyond this and conjectures anything that could be of no use to a player, since it could neither be acted nor have any bearing on the acting, then he is wasting his own time and that of his readers.

This is the test I shall try to apply to my own explanation of Hamlet's delay. Can that explanation be acted, or would it help a player to act the part? Is it not only consistent with the words, but also an elucidation of them? If it is, then I am not passing into irrelevant science because I advance a psychological theory or use psychological terms of which Shakespeare himself was ignorant. As he knew æsthetically what he did not know scientifically, so we may know scientifically what we do not know æsthetically; and we may make use of our science, our psychological formulæ, not to criticize him and find him wanting because he was ignorant of them, but to rediscover that part of his æsthetic purpose which has been lost with the original business of the play. I assume that the character of Hamlet has the consistency of a creation, that Shakespeare knew what he would do and made him do it. If I describe his behaviour in psychological terms, it is not with the aim of travelling beyond the play into speculation about a Hamlet who has no existence, but of discovering how his words ought to be supplemented with action and in what mood he ought to speak them.

Shakespeare's plays can be experienced as he meant them to be experienced only when they are acted. But a performance may be misleading, may cause us actually to read a play wrongly, to ignore some essential point in it which has been ignored in the performance. This I think has happened in the case of

Why Hamlet delayed

Hamlet. In most performances of it that I have seen, the very text, and so the whole part of Hamlet, was misrepresented on an essential point. Hamlet was presented, except for a few unaccountable lapses from decorum and a few regrettable actions still more unaccountable, as a perfectly well-behaved English gentleman; whereas in the text it is all the other way. There Hamlet behaves outrageously except in some of the soliloquies, when he is alone with Horatio, in part of his interview with his mother, and in his converse with the players. In particular, his behaviour to Ophelia is obscene and cruel; and if this is toned down, if his dirty jokes in the play-scene are left out, as they usually are,[1] if his demeanour throughout is far more sympathetic than his actions or his words, then a Hamlet is presented to us who is not Shakespeare's at all, and who is not to be explained in terms either of his words or of his actions.

Yet the text is plain enough; for not only does Hamlet begin to behave wildly immediately after his interview with the Ghost;

---

[1] Of course such jokes were then common; but I do not think the normal Hamlet would have made them to Ophelia.

but, when dying, he insists that all through
the play he has been misexpressing himself;
and his last anxiety is that Horatio shall set
him right with the world—

> Horatio, I am dead ;
> Thou livest ; report me and my cause aright
> To the unsatisfied.

And again, a few lines later—

> O good Horatio, what a wounded name,
> Things standing thus unknown, shall live behind
> me !
> If thou didst ever hold me in thy heart,
> Absent thee from felicity awhile,
> And in this harsh world draw thy breath in pain,
> To tell my story.

His anxiety cannot be merely that Horatio
shall explain the external facts, the murder and
his mother's unfaithfulness, which could be
done in a few words. It is that Horatio shall
make the world understand what he himself,
now that his brain is cleared by approaching
death and a task at last performed, understands
so clearly that he thinks Horatio too must see
it. He cannot tell his story because he is
dying; he has strength only for one practical
task, to recommend Fortinbras for King; and
his last words are—" The rest is silence,"

meaning that he cannot say what he most wishes to say.

So the tragedy and the interest of Hamlet lie in the fact that, by some compulsion, he is forced to misexpress himself in action and in words. What is that compulsion? There has been much speculation about it, as that Hamlet was too much of a dreamer to act when violent action was demanded of him. This ignores the fact that he does act violently throughout the play and it does not explain his outrageous behaviour. It is based upon those very misrepresentations of Hamlet, as a well-behaved English gentleman, which ignore the text; and it is the result of a desire to draw some kind of moral lesson from the play, to prove that all these disasters happened because of some weakness in Hamlet's character. In fact, as Mr. Robertson says, Hamlet has been " scolded, as never hero was before, by literary persons conscious of their own consummate fitness for killing a guilty uncle at a moment's notice." Yet the causes of this compulsion are, I think, made plain in the text and, if once understood by an actor, would show him how to play the part.

Shakespeare's " Hamlet "

The first thing to be noticed in the text is that Hamlet's behaviour, up to his interview with the Ghost, is quite normal. He is aghast, as anyone would be, at his mother's quick remarriage and troubled by doubts about foul play to his father; but, just before the Ghost appears, he is talking calmly about the evils of drunkenness. Further, his behaviour during the interview is also normal, considering the news the Ghost has to tell him. When the Ghost speaks of murder, he says, just what we should expect him to say—

> Haste me to know't, that I, with wings as swift
> As meditation or the thoughts of love,
> May sweep to my revenge.

Those words are the natural prelude to a tragedy of revenge ; yet the tragedy that follows is not one of revenge ; and, as soon as the Ghost has gone, Shakespeare begins that other tragedy which he has designed and which is different from anything that could have been even conceived in the earlier play. For then it is that Hamlet's behaviour begins to be abnormal. He repeats the words—" Remember thee?" and insists on them as if he were already aware of some obstacle to remembrance—

Why Hamlet delayed

Yea, from the table of my memory
I'll wipe away all trivial fond records,
All saws of books, all forms, all pressures past,
That youth and observation copied there ;
And thy commandment all alone shall live
Within the book and volume of my brain,
Unmixed with baser matter : yes, by heaven !
O most pernicious woman !
O villain, villain, smiling, damned villain !
My tables,—meet it is I set it down,
That one may smile, and smile, and be a villain ;
At least I'm sure it may be so in Denmark.
So, uncle, there you are.—Now to my word ;
It is " Adieu, adieu ! remember me " :
I have sworn't.

This, as the rest of the play proves, is not mere
rhetoric ; there is an obstacle to remembrance of
which he speaks afterwards ; and when he writes
on his tables, he is already fighting with it.

It has been pointed out that " table of my
memory " suggests to him his tables or note
books ; and a few lines on there is another
suggestion of the same kind, the mere sameness
of the words carrying his mind from one
thought to another, where there is no other
connexion between them. Horatio cries—
" Illo, ho, ho, my lord ! " and Hamlet answers—
" Hillo, ho, ho, boy ! come, bird, come "; that
is to say, he answers a simple cry as if it

were the cry of a falconer to his birds. This
being at the mercy of words and their chance
suggestions is a symptom of mental disorder ;
and it is the first sign of that disorder in
Hamlet. It may also be a sign of the struggle
for coherence—his mind is in such confusion
that he clutches at any clue to a meaning and
so lets the accidents of language make his
sense for him. All his strange behaviour with
Horatio and Marcellus is of a piece with this.
He speaks " wild and whirling words," in the
hope that the words themselves will express a
purpose or a sense which he cannot find in his
thought. He is on the point of telling the
others what the Ghost has told him and then
flinches from it with the words—

> There's ne'er a villain dwelling in all Denmark—
> But he's an arrant knave—

Something prevents him from telling ; but
it is not policy, it is an obstacle within himself,
a repulsion that he does not understand. And
finally this obstacle becomes for the time his
purpose ; and ·he makes them swear with
desperate particularity that they will be silent
about the whole matter.

Every one to whom the scene is not staled by

Why Hamlet delayed

use must feel the strangeness of it, especially Hamlet's joking with the Ghost; but the strangeness is equalled by the certainty with which it is conceived and executed. It is Shakespeare at the height of his power, setting himself a task of extreme difficulty and performing it as no one else could. But here, if he were influenced by the old play, we should expect to see clearly its influence and its crudity; for the pretended madness of Hamlet is part of the original story and we may assume with Mr. Robertson that it was pretended in the old play, as it is in the German version, to avert the suspicions of the King. Further, madness is very crudely treated in the Elizabethan drama, is often a joke or a mere spectacle, as even in *The Duchess of Malfi*; but here there is no trace of this crudeness or of the old motive except in the words—

> How strange or odd soe'er I bear myself,
> As I perchance hereafter shall think meet
> To put an antic disposition on—

which, as I have said, were probably put in to satisfy those who, remembering the old play, would expect the same pretence of madness in this one, or who might, at least, ask questions

about Hamlet's behaviour. Clearly Shakespeare
has his own new purpose; and what is it?

That, I think, we may learn from the text.
Hamlet is suffering a violent nervous shock
from the Ghost's news, a shock which affects
his behaviour throughout the play; and it is
stressed in this scene as we should expect it to
be, if of so much future importance. Therefore
an actor should stress it in his acting; he should
make us see the nervous shock revealing itself
in Hamlet as soon as the Ghost leaves him.
So, and only so, I think, can he make the scene
intelligible. Hamlet must be "all to pieces"
as his talk and his intentions are all to pieces.

But how does this nervous shock affect him
during the rest of the play? It may be that
we, with our greater psychological knowledge,
can explain that which Shakespeare makes
happen because he knows that it would happen,
better than he could have explained it. Therefore I will venture to apply a psychological
formula to Hamlet. No doubt an expert
psychologist could put it better; but I must
do the best I can, applying to it always this
test—Could it be acted? or would it help a
player to act the part?

Why Hamlet delayed

The formula is this—That when Hamlet was implored by his father's ghost to avenge his murder, and in particular to put an end to the incestuous marriage between his mother and the murderer, his conscious resolve, made with all the force of his will, was to obey his father. But the shock which he suffered on hearing of the murder, and particularly on realizing the full horror of his mother's re-marriage, made, as it were, a wound in his mind, which hurt whenever he thought of the murder, or of his uncle, or of his mother's connexion with his uncle. The pain of the wound was so sharp that, unconsciously, he flinched from it and seized every pretext to forget it. He would will to remember it as he willed to take vengeance; but here "the law of reversed action" worked within him. The more he tried to force himself into action, the more his unconscious invented pretexts why he should delay to act. In fact, the play is made by Hamlet's irrelevance, not by his purpose of revenge. It is the essence of the tragedy that this irrelevance, the result not of any weakness in Hamlet's character but of nervous shock, causes many deaths where there should be only one, and causes Hamlet to misexpress himself in action and in talk. The soliloquies are the great exception. They are far more numerous than in any other of Shakespeare's plays, and they are there to contrast the real with the misexpressed Hamlet and to keep the former in our minds. It is commonly assumed that they are an unnatural device, like arias in an opera; but there are some people who do soliloquize aloud, especially those who are disordered in their minds; and the style of Hamlet's soliloquies is that of a man talking to himself, differing, for the most part, sharply from the style of the more rhetorical passages in the play. An actor could mark this difference; he could lapse into spoken reverie, sometimes brooding, sometimes passionate; and Shakespeare, in one place at least, has insisted how deep this reverie is. For Hamlet is so lost in his first soliloquy—"O! that this too too solid flesh would melt"—that he does not recognize Horatio and then says with a start—" Horatio —or do I forget myself." At least this seems to me the natural dramatic meaning of the passage; though to Mr. Robertson it suggests

Why Hamlet delayed

"long severance." In the soliloquies Hamlet is puzzled by his own behaviour and in them Shakespeare himself insists that that behaviour is abnormal. He must have a purpose in this, artistic and dramatic, not scientific; and that purpose is to represent the complete Hamlet, the Hamlet of his own thoughts as well as the Hamlet who is provoked to excess by people and things. Think of the play without the soliloquies, and you will see that the inner Hamlet is as much a part of the drama as the outer; without the inner, the outer would be the erratic puppet that Mr. Robertson and Mr. Eliot make him out to be.

Mr. Robertson and Mr. Eliot are right when they say that the play deals with the effect of a mother's guilt upon her son, though Mr. Eliot is wrong when he says that that effect cannot be shown in the play. It is shown, whenever Shakespeare wishes to show it, though it is not the whole theme of the play. And no doubt, because the murder of his father is inextricably associated with his mother's guilt, it is repulsive to him, not merely as an act or in its consequences, but as a very subject of thought. That, and not his own wrongs, is

the reason why he hates his uncle so bitterly—
and I have never seen an actor stress this
hatred as much as it is stressed in the text.
Hamlet has, as it were, a "phobia" of the
very subject; merely to think of it brings a
whole train of hideous, uncontrollable associations into his mind, from which he will escape
by any unconscious device.

So much for the formula, which was unknown
to Shakespeare and which, by itself, will not,
of course, account for the effect of the play
upon us. That is produced mainly by Hamlet's
character; and the formula, I would insist,
is not a part of his character but rather a
mechanism to which it is subject and to which
any other character might be subject. The
effect of the play is produced by subjecting
that particular character to that particular
mechanism, though Shakespeare, of course,
never put it so to himself. He saw Hamlet,
with the certainty of intuition, behaving in
a certain way. Perhaps, reading the old play,
he said to himself—" But would a man need to
pretend madness in such a case?" And then,
perhaps, suddenly he saw the whole story in
terms of reality; saw the man of whom that

story might best be told and saw it happening
to him. In most great plays the story is old;
the dramatist shows his genius in discovering
the people of whom it ought to be told; and,
when he has done this, the story becomes his
own and he can make his own play of it.
Then he does not illustrate the story with his
characters; rather they make the story and
make it new; and this is what happened
with Hamlet. Whether he was drawn from
some one whom Shakespeare knew,[1] or from
himself, or from both, or whether he was
conceived because he was the man for that
story, we feel that it could be told about
no one else. Take, for instance, the device
of the play-scene, itself a pretext for escaping
from the task of revenge — Is not Hamlet
the only one of all Shakespeare's tragic
characters to whom that device would be
quite natural? You cannot imagine it
occurring to Othello, or Coriolanus, or Macbeth, or Romeo. Or take the soliloquies
—they must be uttered by a man in the

[1] I have the impression, which, I find, is shared by others,
that Hamlet was drawn from a real man; but, as there is
nothing to prove it, it will not interest a reader who does not
share that impression.

habit of expressing himself to himself, a man
with a gift for expression; and Hamlet has
this beyond any other of Shakespeare's
characters. He is the only one of them, as
Mr. Bradley says, who seems, himself, a man
of genius and who can put his conscious self
before himself with Shakespeare's own power.
The fact that he cannot put his unconscious
self before himself is the tragedy.

Further, for the fullness of the tragedy, there
is needed an incompatibility between the
revenge imposed on Hamlet and his own
character. You can imagine Coriolanus performing that revenge, and probably killing his
mother into the bargain, without hesitation.
But it is not merely pity or gentleness, still
less irresolution, that makes the task distasteful
to Hamlet. He has too rich a nature to be
narrowed into a vendetta; he is interested
in everything, capable of enjoying everything.
Ophelia describes the normal Hamlet when
she says—

Oh, what a noble mind is here o'erthrown !
The courtier's, soldier's, scholar's eye, tongue,
    sword ;
The expectancy and rose of the fair state,
The glass of fashion and the mould of form——

Why Hamlet delayed

And this richness is always rebelling against
the narrow passion of revenge imposed upon
it, and hating the King all the more because
of the alien and importunate hatred that he
inspires; it rebels against the impoverishment,
the obsession, caused by the nervous shock.
Hamlet would be doing so many things; and
he is forced to be thinking of only one thing
and that a thing contrary to his own nature.
The tragedy would be far less if Othello were
the hero of it; just as, if Hamlet had been
Desdemona's husband, that tragedy would
never have happened.

Nor would the tragedy of Hamlet have
happened if he had been merely an amiable
character of weak will; it does happen because
the machinery of a strong will is disordered;
and it is the contrast between the will and
its disordered machinery which makes both the
interest and the pity of the play. Hamlet
would be a dazzling character in a comedy;
but in his own play he has the beauty and
pathos of a sick child as well; he is more fully
revealed than he could be otherwise; he is
in fact the man for the part.

All this is beyond the formula; yet the

formula may help us to see it; it may discover for us the underlying logic of certain
scenes which might otherwise seem exhibitions
of mere comic caprice, and which often are
so acted. There is, for instance, Hamlet's behaviour to Polonius, half comic, half pathetic.
With Polonius he does put on an antic
disposition, which is provoked by the fact
that Polonius assumes him to be mad. In
the first interview (Act II. Scene II.) Polonius
says to him—"Do you know me, my lord?"
and Hamlet plays up to the question by
answering—"Excellent well; you are a fishmonger." We must all have wished we could
enjoy the licence of madness when pestered by
some eminent bore, and Charles Lamb took that
licence; his behaviour to the man who asked
Wordsworth whether he did not think Milton a
great poet was like the behaviour of Hamlet
to Polonius. "I must feel that gentleman's
bumps," he cried, and had to be removed to
Haydon's studio. But Polonius, besides being
a bore incapable of understanding Hamlet,
sane or mad, is a further source of disturbance
to him in that he is Ophelia's father. Ophelia
attracts and repels him for reasons which I

will try to give when I come to the scene
between her and Hamlet; she is closely,
though accidentally, associated with his main
trouble; and Polonius is incongruously associated with her. Thus Hamlet does harp on
Ophelia to Polonius, as Polonius remarks,
though not for the simple reason that he is
in love with her. In the interview with
Polonius Shakespeare proves how closely he
has observed melancholy, in himself or in
others. Hamlet is fighting his melancholy
while he trifles with Polonius; but twice he
slips back into it with the irrelevant, sighed,
or groaned, exclamations of a melancholiac.
When Polonius asks him fussily—" Will you
walk out of the air, my lord?" he answers—
" Into my grave?" And when Polonius says—
" I will most humbly take my leave of you,"
he replies—" You cannot, sir, take from me
anything that I will more willingly part
withal; except my life, except my life, except
my life." The repetition here is a symptom of
mechanical falling back into a persistent state
of melancholy.

And then follows the scene with Rosencrantz
and Guildenstern, a scene such as no dramatist

had ever written before and none has ever
equalled since; for it is the dramatization of
a disordered state of mind, the exhibition of it,
not in analysis or soliloquy, but in dialogue
never forced and remaining relevant to the
play. This scene, to be acted intelligibly,
must be understood; and the psychological
formula will, I think, help us to understand
every turn of it.

Remember that Hamlet, unconsciously, is
seeking every pretext to escape from the
thought of the murder and his mother's unfaithfulness, and that everything associated
with these subjects is painful to him; everything connected with the court, for instance,
for the court centres in the King and Queen.
Rosencrantz and Guildenstern are free from
these associations, for they have only just
returned to the court; and he welcomes them
as a diversion from Polonius, one of " these
tedious old fools" who belong to the weari-
some and horrible world of the court. What
Hamlet desires in his trouble is disinterested
friends, like Horatio, not tainted by dull and
wicked worldliness—friends who will seem to
belong to his own happy, unwounded past.

Why Hamlet delayed

He takes Rosencrantz and Guildenstern to be such—"My excellent good friends! How dost thou, Guildenstern?—Ah, Rosencrantz? Good lads, how do ye both?" and in this warmth we can see him insisting to himself that they are what he would have them be, good lads, belonging to the past of friendship and freedom. But they do not answer in his mood—the contrast could, and should, be marked in the acting — there is all the disguised caution of the court in their reply—

> *R.* As the indifferent children of the earth.
> *G.* Happy in that we are not over-happy ;
> On Fortune's cap we are not the very button.

And instantly Hamlet is on his guard too. "Nor the soles of her shoe?" he says, and then makes a dirty joke, as being the kind of conversation fit for courtiers. They continue the joke and so fall more and more into the "complex" of the court for him ; and the suspicion grows in him that they have come with an object. What he longs for is friends without an object. "Let me question you more in particular," he says. "What have you, my good friends, deserved at the hands of Fortune, that she sends you to prison hither?"

Prison means for him the prison of his own mind, the complex into which they now are drawn. It is not a prison to them, they say; and he remarks how he is divided from them by his state of mind—"There is nothing either good or bad, but thinking makes it so; to me it is a prison." And then Rosencrantz, cunningly but insensitively, begins to probe him, suggesting that ambition makes Denmark a prison to him. Hamlet sees that the mis-understanding is complete—that anyone should suspect him of ambition of all things! "O God, I could be bounded in a nut-shell, and count myself a king of infinite space, were it not that I have had dreams."[1] Then, in his weariness, he is drawn into a passage of aimless wit which he ends by saying—"Shall we to the court? for, by my fay, I cannot reason." The court and court-formulæ are the only things for them. They say together eagerly yet obsequiously, like two designing court-puppets, "We'll wait upon you"; and again

---

[1] It seems to me that the emendation here of *had* for *bad* is proved right by the context.

Why Hamlet delayed

Hamlet tries to turn them into friends—"No such matter; I will not sort you with the rest of my servants; for, to speak to you like an honest man, I am most dreadfully attended." Then suspicion possesses him again, and he asks—"But, in the beaten way of friendship, what make you at Elsinore?" They lie and he knows they lie—"To visit you, my lord; no other occasion"; and then his suspicion bursts out, still in conflict with his desire for friendship. "Were you not sent for? Is it your own inclining? Is it a free visitation? Come, deal justly with me; come, come; nay, speak." They can say anything but to the purpose, the purpose being that they shall convince him of their friendship. And then he puts his suspicion to them directly—"I know the good King and Queen have sent for you." Still they fence with him—"To what end, my lord?" And again he makes a yet wilder appeal that they shall be Horatios to him. "By the rights of our fellowship, by the consonancy of our youth, by the obligation of our ever-preserved love, and by what more dear a better proposer could charge you withal, be even and direct with me, whether you were sent for, or no." They whisper fatally together, but then have the wit to confess they were sent for; and Hamlet, melted by this one piece of honesty, like a neurasthenic cannot forbear from telling them about the state of his own mind; only few neurasthenics can describe themselves so. He tells how his distaste, caused, though he does not know it, by the crime of the King and Queen, has spread to everything; and at the same time he shows us what a love of life that distaste has infected and perverted. Then, at the end, there is a sudden return of suspicion—— " Man delights not me, no, nor woman neither, though by your smiling you seem to say so."

Then come the players, another diversion. They are outside the complex, but they are drawn into it; for they suggest to him a pretext by which he shall yet again put off his revenge, while seeming to advance it. In the soliloquy—" Oh, what a rogue and peasant slave am I!"—he begins by contrasting the player's emotion over an imaginary sorrow with his own failure even to feel what he should, with his strange and persistent irrelevance. So he incites his conscious desire for revenge; but, out of that very incitement, comes another pretext for delay suggested by his unconscious; the spirit he has seen may be the devil and may have deceived him; he must have a proof of the King's guilt and the play will give it to him.

Now I do not say that all this can be acted; but I believe that, by means of it, an actor could give meaning and consistency to the part of Hamlet. If Hamlet is merely comic in his scenes with Polonius, merely rhetorical in his soliloquies or in his account of his melancholy to Rosencrantz and Guildenstern, then it is but a part "with a lot of fat" in it; and one might indeed believe that Shakespeare had taken an old and crude play, kept its essential crudity, but made a fine talkative Hamlet for Burbage to display himself in. The play, as often acted, is like a concerto composed for a virtuoso pianist, with no logic of construction but plenty of showy passages for the piano. Many actors, famous in their day, have played it so; but, though there is Elizabethan rhetoric in it, if Hamlet plays his part rhetorically, he makes nonsense of it. He himself gives warning on this point, in his

advice to the players, which should be applied
to his own part. " There be players that I have
seen play and heard others praise . . . that
have so strutted and bellowed that I have
thought some of nature's journeymen had
made men and not made them well, they
imitated humanity so abominably." If you
are to imitate humanity well, you must have
something to imitate, just as if you are to
play music well you must have real music
to play. The scene with Rosencrantz and
Guildenstern is not merely words to be
bellowed, nor is it merely character to be
displayed ; it is character subject to a particular
psychological state which governs all its
changes of mood ; and it is in this counter-
point of character and psychological state that
the main interest of the play lies. It would
be possible, as it is necessary, to act Hamlet's
eagerness of welcome to Rosencrantz and
Guildenstern, and their easy yet mechanical
response to it ; to show his instant change
of mood, falling in with theirs, his growing
suspicion heightened by their hint about
ambition, and then his sudden return to his
first eagerness, now become desperate because

it is sure of disappointment; and then again the intensity with which he describes his melancholy and tries to make them understand, what he cannot, why his distaste has spread to all the things he loves most, while for the moment he loses it in the very description of all that he has ceased to care for. It would be possible to act all this, but only if the actor saw the meaning of it all; and the easiest way to this meaning, now, is by psychology.

It is to be noted that Hamlet welcomes the players as eagerly as he had welcomed Rosencrantz and Guildenstern—" You are welcome, masters; welcome all. I am glad to see thee well; welcome, good friends. O, my old friend! Why thy face is valanced, since I saw thee last; comest thou to beard me in Denmark?—What, my young lady and mistress! By'r lady, your ladyship is nearer to heaven than when I saw you last by the altitude of a chopine. . . ." They at least have nothing to do with the court and they bring his free past back to him. Happy for the moment in this freedom, so that he may keep it, he cries— " We'll have a speech straight; come, give us a taste of your quality; come, a passionate speech."

As important as the scene with Rosencrantz and Guildenstern is the scene with Ophelia; and, unless an actor understands this, and acts his understanding, he will make it merely mad and repulsive. The prelude to this scene is "To be or not to be," in which Hamlet is brooding more aimlessly than ever. Already he has lost the eagerness which the device of the play-scene had given him for a moment; he has forgotten all about his father's Ghost, and seems to be so far in unconscious doubt about it that he speaks of the "undiscovered country from whose bourn no traveller returns." This may be Shakespeare's inadvertence but it is more likely Hamlet's oblivion. He is just speaking in general terms of how the native hue of resolution is sicklied o'er with the pale cast of thought, being so deep in his own state that he presents it to himself as universal, when he sees Ophelia. For the moment his past again rushes back to him, and he addresses her like a rapturous yet courtly lover—

> Nymph, in thy orisons
> Be all my sins remembered—

addresses her in fact as he had addressed her
in the letter which Polonius reads to the King
and Queen. Until the interview with the
Ghost, he had been quite simply and without
misgiving in love with her. It is the interview
with the Ghost which changes his behaviour
towards her, for reasons which I will now give.

Ophelia, while she recalls the past to him, is
also horribly connected with the present. She
is a woman like his mother, and also a woman
of the court; and in the past he had loved
her as he loved his mother. If we would
explain the shock which his mother's adultery
had given him in psychological terms, we may
say that, having thought of her entirely as a
mother, he found something vilely incongruous
in her renewing of her sexual youth with his
uncle, especially as his uncle had become
physically loathsome to him. He can no
longer think of her as his mother; she has
become something else to him; and his mind
is made sick and dizzy by the change of
associations.

Further, it is a fact that men of delicate
spirit expect and find something maternal in
the women they fall in love with. The phrase

" Œdipus complex " is now used to describe this association; but it suggests something un- natural and unhealthy, whereas the association itself is not only natural and healthy but an element in all love that is not mere desire. Men get an idea of woman from their mothers, and fall in love with women in whom they recognize the same idea. They are truly in love with an incarnation of the divine and universal woman. But, if a man's idea of his mother were suddenly destroyed, as Hamlet's was, by her adultery, the association between her and the woman he loved would be likely to infect his love with his disgust for his mother. So Hamlet, having seen his mother in Ophelia, still sees her, horribly changed, in Ophelia; and his anger with his mother involves her.

You may think this too fanciful; but the text bears it out and there is no other explana- tion of his sudden change of manner to Ophelia. She herself incites it by her provocative remark—

How does your honour for this many a day?— implying that lately she has seen less of him than before; and still more by returning her

Why Hamlet delayed

presents, which no doubt, he imputes to her father's orders. "I never gave you aught," he says, meaning that he revokes his past love and all dealings between them. And then suspicion breaks into words, as with Rosencrantz and Guildenstern. "Are you fair? Are you honest?" But, in the midst of his cruel banter he remembers—"I did love you once"; and then follows a proof how much his mother is in his mind. "You should not have believed me; for virtue cannot so inoculate our old stock but we shall relish of it. I loved you not." He must be as faithless as his mother, he means; she had seemed to love his father. But, if he is doomed to be faithless, Ophelia had better have nothing to do with men. So he tells her to go to a nunnery. For the moment he has transferred the conviction of sexual sin from her to himself, because he is the son of his mother—"I could accuse myself of such things, that it were better my mother had not borne me." And then gradually he falls more and more into a rage with Ophelia because he loves her still and because she is so meek. But his rage against her is his rage against his mother, whom he also loves, and he expresses it in abuse of all women of the court, who cannot be themselves, who must paint and amble and jig and lisp and talk hidden obscenities. All that he says is the very opposite of the truth about Ophelia, but that is why he says it. As with Rosencrantz and Guildenstern, he grows more and more desperately serious, as if hoping that she will be provoked into some reassuring defiance. But that is beyond her, which is her tragedy, and the tragedy of Hamlet's loneliness. His mother has failed him and Ophelia seems to fail him too; they are both of the court, of this world of murder and adultery and complying insincerity; even the woman he loves is of it; and all the while she is simply bewildered and frightened.

So in the next scene, after his advice to the players, he turns passionately to Horatio as one who is not of the court nor yet passion's slave like himself. All his affection, which has recoiled baffled from Ophelia, tries now to satisfy itself with Horatio; and it is again part of the tragedy that Horatio, with all his virtues, is not understanding. Shakespeare has conceived him for his part in the tragedy

Why Hamlet delayed

as surely as Hamlet himself. We may find no fault in him; but in Hamlet's affection for him and his temperate response to it, as if he were a kind of George Washington, we feel Hamlet's loneliness still more keenly.

The scene with Ophelia is merely painful and unintelligible unless the actor can show that Hamlet is misexpressing himself under a compulsion he does not understand. He must act his nervous instability and express it in every change of mood; or Hamlet will be only a brutal buffoon.

In the play-scene Ophelia attracts and repels him to further outrage all the more outrageous because it is before the whole court. If his obscenities are left out, as they usually are, the edge of the tragedy is blunted. Hamlet treats Ophelia before the court as one of the court, and the court should laugh at his dirty jokes. Ophelia herself hardly resents them; she is trying to do her duty by every one and she does not know what her duty to Hamlet may be.

Through the play-scene his excitement and his spirits rise continually. It seems to him that he is really doing something at last, when the players are doing it. Then, when the King has fled proving his guilt, he springs triumphant on to the stage and shouts his irrelevant verses; but instantly the tide begins to turn and he says ironically—"Would not this get me a fellowship in a cry of players?" He sees that what has been done is but play-acting; the King has been frighted, but with false fire.

Then in the following scene with Rosencrantz and Guildenstern Hamlet has forgotten the play and his task and everything practical in a dramatic performance of his own with the recorders. He is here at the height of his powers, as if he were Shakespeare himself presented on the stage; but his triumph is one of art not of fact. His unconscious has turned him from the ugly world of fact into this other world of art where he can forget it for the moment.

It would be mere ingenuity, I think, to explain Hamlet's refusal to kill the King at his prayers as yet another trick of his unconscious finding any pretext to turn him from his task. In this case the explanation could not be acted and so would, I believe, be wrong. It may be that, in fact, a man such as Hamlet would find a pretext for refusing to kill his enemy in such a case; but the text here gives no hint of it. The explanation both of Hamlet's refusal and of Shakespeare's intention, is, I think, much simpler. What Hamlet really expresses in the scene is his extreme hatred of the King, upon which the text insists again and again. It is a physical as well as moral loathing, caused no doubt by the thought of the King's adultery with his mother. Here, above all, we have to rid our minds of the notion of a gentle, dreaming Hamlet. Hamlet does really wish to catch the King "in the incestuous pleasure of his bed"; he does wish to enjoy the pleasure of killing him; and he must be in a rage to do that, which he cannot be while the King is meekly kneeling upon his knees. The only way Hamlet can bring himself to think of revenge at all, associated as it is with the thought of his father's murder and his mother's adultery, is by working himself up into a rage with the murderer and adulterer. In this scene we should see him trying to do that and failing while the King prays before him.

This, I think, could be acted, so as to make even the theological scruple seem natural to us; but it is, for a modern audience, the most

difficult scene in the play because the feelings
of Hamlet would not now express themselves
in a theological formula. It is probable that
Shakespeare kept that formula from the older
play, since it is in the German version ; but he
has used it for his own purposes and adjusted
it to the character of his Hamlet.

The first point to be noted about the scene
between Hamlet and his mother is that almost
throughout he behaves normally. Even the
sudden stabbing of Polonius through the arras
is what we should expect from the scene before.
Hamlet would not kill the King praying but
he is ready enough to kill him eavesdropping ;
indeed he could not find a better way of killing
a man whom he loathed so much that he did
not care to touch him even with a sword,
than to stab him through a curtain. The
words—" How now ! a rat ? dead, for a ducat,
dead ! " express the feeling with which he would
wish to kill the King—as if he were vermin and,
like vermin, skulking behind hangings. It is
not natural to Hamlet to kill men, nor can he
take any primitive pleasure in it ; and this
scene refutes once and for all the notion of
some critics that he wished to make of his

revenge a solemn act of justice. What he does wish is to get the King out of the way and then forget about him; and this wish is so strong that he is ready to kill him even in his mother's presence.

The scene begins a little theatrically as if Shakespeare had not, at this moment, a very firm grasp of Hamlet's behaviour—Hamlet is best revealed either in intimate talk or in that fantastic behaviour which expresses a thwarted desire for intimacy. To his mother he cannot be either intimate or fantastic. So Shakespeare falls back upon the splendid rhetoric which is his usual resource when at a loss. He insists upon Hamlet's physical loathing of the King and upon his horror of his mother's adultery directly and in language which is not peculiarly Hamlet's. Some of this scene seems written to make things clear to the stupider part of his audience.

It is curious that the Ghost should appear saying—

> Do not forget : this visitation
> Is but to whet thy almost blunted purpose—

when Hamlet has just killed Polonius in mistake for the King. We may find ingenious explanations of this inconsistency; but here I suspect a survival from the old play. Shakespeare would consent to it because we do not notice the inconsistency when we see the scene acted, and because the Ghost's appearance, at this point, and in the presence of Gertrude though unseen by her, is most effective theatrically. Further, it has the dramatic effect of changing Hamlet's mood to his mother; for the Ghost says—

> But look, amazement on thy mother sits;
> Oh, step between her and her fighting soul.
> Conceit in weakest bodies strongest works;
> Speak to her, Hamlet.

And from this point Hamlet's manner to her is both kinder and more intimate. He is himself, and not merely a splendid speech-maker, in the passage—" My pulse, as yours, doth temperately keep time "; though he goes off into bitterness again when he thinks of her sharing the King's bed.

Hamlet here insists upon his sanity in a manner which proves that Shakespeare wished to insist upon it; and his sanity here is what we should expect, because, though he is face to face with the subject of his horror, he is able

Why Hamlet delayed

to express that horror to one of the persons who have caused it. This talking to his mother, like the play-scene, is for him an action which for the moment sets his spirit free. Instead of killing the King, he can talk about the King to her, a much more natural way, for him, of venting his hate. Those critics who reproach him for preferring words to acts forgot that it is a mark of civilization, not of weak will, to prefer words to acts of violence. Hamlet's desire is to change the mind of his mother; and he would, no doubt, if he thought it possible, try to change the mind of the King. What infuriates men like Hamlet in men like the King is the fact that their minds cannot be changed; that is why they seem to be vermin, but killing is no remedy for the fact that vermin in human shape exist.

Hamlet's behaviour to Rosencrantz and Guildenstern, and to the King, when questioned about Polonius, is an echo of his behaviour after his first interview with the Ghost and, like that, a reaction after nervous shock. It would be repulsive, if an actor playing it did not show the symptoms of nervous shock. But

the moment the King tells him he is to go to
England, the symptoms disappear. It is a
practical diversion; something to be done and
experienced which takes him away from his
horror. His last words are—

> Father and mother is man and wife: man and
> wife is one flesh; and so, my mother. Come, for
> England!

It is because the King and his mother are one
flesh that he would rather escape from them
than take revenge; killing is no remedy for that.

And then follows the scene in which Hamlet
hears of the expedition of Fortinbras to Poland
and contrasts the activity of Fortinbras with
his own inaction. In this soliloquy his be-
wilderment at the processes of his own mind is
clearly expressed. Nowhere else is there such
rambling of thought, as if the conscious were
feeling about for a cause which remains in the
unconscious; or such argument about himself,
as if that self were something not himself
which he can observe but not control. Here
he insists that there are no external obstacles
to his revenge—

> Sith I have cause, and will, and strength, and
>   means,
> To do't——

Why Hamlet delayed

And here he speaks of bestial oblivion, really the shrinking of his unconscious from the very subject of revenge, which expresses itself, to the conscious, in forgetfulness. Talking of Fortinbras, he tries to feel like Fortinbras, to dramatize himself as Fortinbras—

> Rightly to be great
> Is not to stir without great argument,
> But greatly to find quarrel in a straw,
> When honour's at the stake.

That is the more primitive kind of man that Hamlet, for the moment, would be, just as he had wished to be Horatio. But he cannot be either. He hates but with a hatred that cannot be satisfied with any act of revenge, since it is really not so much hatred even of the King as of a beastliness in life itself which the King represents for him. That is what is meant when Hamlet is called a philosopher. It is not that he is incapable of action but that action cannot satisfy a mind shocked by life itself. If he kills the King, he will not kill that beastliness, which, since the King and Queen first convinced him of it, have infected the whole of his world so that Denmark is to him a prison. It is like shell-shock, which establishes such a tyranny over the mind that little noises shock it like the shell. So Hamlet scents lust even in Ophelia, and the King's cold, murderous policy in all the courtiers. Not one of them will ever say the thing he means, for their meaning is always furtive and evil; and so he does not feel much regret over killing Polonius, who was eavesdropping like a courtier.

> The time is out of joint :—O cursed spite,
> That ever I was born to set it right !

That was his conclusion after he had heard of the murder of his father. All things, not merely the King and Queen, are wrong; so he will hail any chance of escaping from this world where beastliness reigns; he is like a neurasthenic who thinks that change of place will mean change of mind.

Hamlet's absence is convenient to the actor who plays the part, for it gives him a rest which he must need. It also gives the audience a relaxation from the exacting task of following all his subtleties; and, in the fifth act, he returns with all the more effect. This is enough, I think, to explain why Shakespeare

Why Hamlet delayed

dispatched him, making use, no doubt, of a crude device in the old play. Its crudity does not matter since it is not inconsistent with Hamlet's character, but rather natural to his mood, that he should seize any pretext for escaping. And then reappearing in the Grave-digger's scene he is drawn artfully and gradually into the action of the play. He does not return hot for revenge, but will talk of anything and particularly of the manners of courtiers— "This might be my Lord Such-an-one that praised my Lord Such-an-one's horse, when he meant to beg it, might it not?"

At the beginning of this scene **Hamlet** seems dazed and aimless, ready to talk of the aimless indignity of death—"How long will a man lie i' the earth ere he will rot?" He comes back for a moment to himself in his memories of Yorick; but then talks of dissolution like Donne himself; one might indeed suspect that Donne remembered him in at least one famous passage of his sermons. But he is brought into the action again with Ophelia's funeral and with his own words—

But soft, but soft! aside: here comes the King.

Nowhere does he behave so outrageously as
when he leaps into the grave where Laertes is
mouthing grief and vengeance together. It is
like Hamlet, as Mr. Bradley has remarked, to
be thus æsthetically provoked by the manner
in which Laertes exploits the situation. Adopt-
ing the same manner, dramatizing himself as
Laertes, as before he had dramatized himself as
Fortinbras, he cries—

> This is I,
> Hamlet, the Dane.

Nothing can be more theatrically effective—
for those who see Hamlet as melodrama; but
it is also satire on the natural staginess of
people like Laertes, and satire natural to
Hamlet. His impatience with Laertes is an
echo of his impatience with the player. " Begin
murderer ; pox, leave thy damnable faces, and
begin." He does not believe in love that can
express itself thus ; and, seeing Ophelia's grave,
he is aware that he loved her, though he cannot
express his love with Laertes ranting there
before the King—

> I loved Ophelia ; forty thousand brothers
> Could not, with all their quantity of love,
> Make up my sum—What wilt thou do for her ?

Why Hamlet delayed

Then follows a series of protestations with the sudden ending

> Nay, and thou'lt mouth,
> I'll rant as well as thou.

It is part of his trouble that he cannot express any of his most real feelings directly; when he would say that he loved Ophelia, he must parody her brother. He regrets it afterwards; but even then he adds—

> But, sure, the bravery of his grief did put me
> Into a towering passion.

The last of Hamlet's antic disposition is seen in his dialogue with Osric, again an echo of the scenes with Rosencrantz and Guildenstern; for Osric, with his airs and graces, also makes him think of the court and sets him jangling out of tune. He parodies Osric to his face as he parodied Laertes; and he enjoys doing it, for again it is art which diverts him from reality. There is nothing Hamlet hates more than fashion for its own sake; and those who tell us that Shakespeare was a snob in his ridicule of the mob forgot that there is far more bitterness in his ridicule of courtiers. He has the artist's dislike for all kinds of unreality, whether it be a crowd shouting at the word of command

or a courtier talking court-jargon. The little
scene between Hamlet and Horatio before the
fencing has in it the last touch of his melancholy
with the sudden change to a sigh—" I shall win
at the odds. But thou wouldst not think how ill
all's here about my heart; but it is no matter."

And then follows the sense of destiny to be
fulfilled at last—" If it be now, 'tis not to
come: if it be not to come, it will be now: if
it be not now, yet it will come; the readiness
is all; since no man has aught of what he
leaves, what is it to leave betimes? Let be."

Asking pardon of Laertes, he is for the first
time, before the court, an accomplished gentleman. He even pleads his own madness, or
distraction; and here, if this change be well
acted, we cannot but feel the end approaching.
Laertes, like the young pedant that he is, says
he must bring his cause before a court of
honour; and Hamlet plays up to his gallantries
with compliments that still seem to have a
hint of irony in them—

> I'll be your foil, Laertes; in mine ignorance
> Your skill shall, like a star i' the darkest night,
> Stick fiery off indeed.

It is a politeness almost Chinese; and, another

ominous sign, he is now ceremoniously polite to the King also. Then the end comes with a rush; and, even when the King and Hamlet are both dying, he remembers the King's worst offence, his adultery with the Queen—

> Here, thou incestuous, murderous, damned Dane,
> Drink off this potion! Is thy union here?
> Follow my mother.

Then, the King being dead, he thinks no more of him. Dying himself, his last desire is that Horatio shall set him right with the world. The play ends with this desire unfulfilled; and the entry of Fortinbras tells that it is over and that life remains for good, commonplace people, such as Horatio, who certainly cannot explain Hamlet.

The end is sudden; but the reader must remember that it was written to be acted, and that actors can lay an emphasis which will give weight to a scene that seems too swift and light when read. The nature of the plot is such that the end could not be prepared or foreseen long beforehand. It must come of events which force Hamlet to act on the spur of the moment. The play is bitter tragedy through-out, perhaps the bitterest of all tragedies, but

it is not gloomy, because of the brilliance and
diversity of Hamlet's mind, because he is
always his own Mercutio. He flashes and
dances through a hideous world which heightens
his beauty by contrast; and that beauty is
the theme and the justification of the play.

CHAPTER III

On " Hamlet " as an Æsthetic Document

THE reader is now, I hope, convinced that *Hamlet* is a good play, if he needed convincing; but I have not written at this length only to convince him. I have wished to deal with two kinds of criticism which seem to me perverse though common; and to examine *Hamlet* in detail as being an important document for all who would understand the nature, not only of dramatic art, but of all art. When Mr. Robertson says that *Hamlet* is to be understood only in terms of some earlier play, I would answer—" Then it cannot be worth understanding"; and Mr. Eliot implies that it is not worth understanding, when he says that it is most certainly an artistic failure. To him I am provoked to reply—" But it is one of the documents from which we may learn what artistic success is."

To deny that is to ignore the facts of art for a theory which will land you at last on some desert absurdity—as that *Coriolanus* is a better play than *Hamlet*.

Such criticism, especially if practised with an intimidating manner, sets up obstructions to the experience of works of art, which it is one of the main functions of criticism to remove. We are all subject to wrong suggestions about works of art as about other things; and the critic helps us if he can rid our minds of them so that we may experience works of art simply. There are, for instance, the suggestions likely to affect the ordinary man, which are usually wrong expectations. He expects all works of art to be like those to which he is accustomed; he expects to be amused at once, and without any effort on his part, by every work of art; and, if he is not, he decides that it is not for him. But there are also other, less crude and less obviously wrong, suggestions. For instance, the suggestions of learning, that a work of art is to be studied mainly as a historical document or as a link in some process of evolution; or else, if it be a tragedy, that we must examine

84

it to see how far it conforms to the principles laid down by Aristotle in his *Poetics* or by any other critic in whom we trust. And, finally, there are the suggestions of fastidiousness, which come of our anxiety not to like anything we ought not to like, or of a mechanical reaction against what is commonly said. All of these are obstructions; and criticism should set us on our guard against them.

Aristotle's *Poetics* were long an obstruction to the experience of dramatic art, often because they were misunderstood, and often because it was forgotten that Aristotle had but a short and limited experience of that art. When we read *The Poetics*, we should remember that he wrote them without knowing *Hamlet*, and that, if he had known it, he might have written them differently; for he was a great man who would rather learn from facts than deny them. *Hamlet* is an important æsthetic document because its method is not one known to Aristotle, because it is something added by Shakespeare to the resources of his art. The law of art is all case-law, and *Hamlet* is a case that has been decided in the court of experience.

Shakespeare's " Hamlet "

If Aristotle had read the plot of *Hamlet* in a bald outline he might well have condemned it; whereas, if he had read the plot of *Coriolanus*, he might have thought it all that a dramatist could wish for. But, in fact, plots in a bald outline are nothing; and criticism based on an examination and classification of them is nothing. Aristotle says that plot is the soul of tragedy, which should imply that the soul cannot be separated from the body; the plot cannot be related in other words, for, if it is, it is no longer the plot. But even Aristotle seems near to error when he says that plot is the principal part of tragedy, and character the part next in rank; for the better a tragedy, is the less possible is it to separate character from plot. What is done is done by particular persons, and what happens happens to them; it would be all different and perhaps absurd if the characters were different. If we can make a distinction between plot and character, the play falls short of complete success. We can make that distinction, to some extent, in *Coriolanus*; we can consider the plot apart from the characters without feeling that we are doing something very foolish; but in *Hamlet* we cannot. The plot of that play is what it is because Hamlet is what he is; apart from him, there is no meaning or coherence in it, and it does seem a plot for Kyd rather than for Shakespeare.

Aristotle, again, says that a plot is not one merely because the hero is one. Numberless events happen to any man, many of which cannot be connected into one event; and there are many actions of one man which cannot be connected into a single action. So the poet should choose for his plot only those events which can be connected into one event and those actions which can be connected into one action. To this we must agree; there must be some kind of unity in a plot; but what is the nature of the connexion in *Hamlet* which gives unity to the plot? That we must seek in *Hamlet* and not in Aristotle; for it is, I think, a connexion which Aristotle had not experienced in any Greek play, and which therefore he has not mentioned. Yet it does give unity to the plot, and a unity perhaps more complete than is to be found in any other play whatever.

Shakespeare's " Hamlet "

Even Mr. Eliot says that in Shakespeare's
Hamlet there is an "unmistakable tone"
which is "unmistakably not in the earlier
play." About the earlier play I, like Mr. Eliot,
know nothing ; but I agree that the peculiarity
of *Hamlet* is in its tone, though not that the
tone can be separated from the action.
Rather I insist that the action is unified by
the tone, which all comes from Hamlet himself. The peculiarity of the play consists,
first, in this, that its unity is given to it by
the predominance of a single character, a predominance so great that we see all the other
characters only in relation to Hamlet and as
contrasts to him at one point or another.
Now you may say, if you please, that this
ought not to be done ; only Shakespeare has
done it. And he has done another thing, still
more surprising, which seems contrary to the
principles of Aristotle. It is not only the
character of Hamlet that makes the unity
of the play ; but it is also a particular, and
morbid, state of that character ; for without
the shock suffered by Hamlet, and the con-
sequent disorder of his mind, the plot would
lack all reason and coherence.

As an Æsthetic Document

Aristotle lays it down that the hero of a tragedy should be involved in misfortune, not through his deliberate vice or villainy, but through some error of human frailty. The word ἁμαρτία used here by Aristotle has been explained as meaning either a fault through avoidable or excusable ignorance, or one incurred through passion but without evil will. In fact Aristotle holds that in Tragedy there should be some justification of the ways of God to man, or of the order of things. If misfortunes happen, they should happen through the hero's own fault, which, yet, should not be so great as to deprive him of our sympathy. But Hamlet's misfortune does not happen to him either through avoidable ignorance or through passion. It happens, in the first place, because of crimes in which he is not implicated at all, and, in the second, through the nervous shock which he suffers on hearing of those crimes, and which is great, not because of the weakness, but because of the beauty of his nature. We should think poorly of a man who did not suffer so in such a case. In fact the key to this tragedy is to be

89

found in the words of Ophelia, not of Aristotle—

> Now see that noble and most sovereign reason
> Like sweet bells jangled out of tune and harsh.

It is something which happens to Hamlet, not something done by him, that causes all the disaster; though, as Mr. Robertson says, critics, no doubt remembering Aristotle or governed by his desire to justify the ways of God to man, have often preached to Hamlet, like his comforters to Job.

Again, we may say that a tragedy ought not to be made out of the undeserved suffering of the hero, or, in particular, out of his mental disorder; only, again, Shakespeare has done it. We might expect that a tragedy so made would be merely disagreeable; Mr. Eliot seems to think it is. " Shakespeare," he says, " attempted to express the inexpressibly horrible," and failed. He implies, in fact, that the tragedy lacks beauty, when beauty is its most signal and most surprising quality. That is why *Hamlet* is an important æsthetic document. Beauty is achieved where we should not expect it to be achieved; and how?

As an Æsthetic Document

I cannot attempt to answer this question without also attempting a statement of first principles, for which I ask the reader's patience.

All art is an expression of values; but the expression of values does not mean the statement of them. I may say what I value and leave every one cold; but values are expressed when they are communicated—that is to say, when the artist, by means of his work of art, causes his audience to share them. Unless this happens, unless the values are communicated, they are not expressed for the audience. The artist, however, has no practical purpose in the communication of his values; he does not attempt it either because he wishes to make his audience better men or because he hopes to get anything by it. Rather the desire to express, to communicate, is itself a part of that kind of experience which we call valuing; *the experience itself is not complete without expression.* Further, valuing is not merely moral, as we know in the case of love. It is an experience, always emotional and recognized by the emotion which accompanies it, an experience of which the immediate issue is simply the impulse to expression and communication. Art, in fact, is the practical result of it; whenever we have the emotion of value, we are, potentially, artists. But the emotion, if it cannot find expression, is incomplete and baulked; if it produces only a direct statement of values, it has not expressed, or communicated itself. Indeed, art cannot be a mere statement of values; the artist gives us something that is not an opinion, in which we see no opinion at all; he can express his values only in some *object*, which, without our knowing it, makes us value what he values; and this object he produces without making a statement of his values even to himself.

Thus, in music there can be no statement of values, for it is incapable of making any statement whatever; and the musician himself would be unable to say in words what values he had expressed in his music. Music is the object in which he expresses and communicates them; and our sense of the beauty of music is our sense of those values. And so it is with all the arts; when we are aware of beauty in them, then the artist has communicated his values to us; and, the more successful the process of communication, the less are we

aware of it. We do not say—" I value this
or that "—but only—" This is beautiful." We
are, however, aware of differences in the quality
of beauty ; and these correspond to differences
in the quality of the values communicated.
Beauty seems to us profound, and is most
permanent in its effects upon us, when the
artist has communicated to us his deepest and
most permanent values, those which he has
acquired through his most intense and complete experience. So, the quality of a man's
art, given that he is an artist at all, depends
upon his experiencing power. There are real
artists, who give us a real, though slight,
beauty, because their experiencing power is
slight and their values, quick perhaps and
vivid, are for little things. We are aware of
this difference, as a difference in the quality
of beauty, very clearly in music. For instance,
the melodies of Sullivan are real melodies ; but
their beauty, which is also real, expresses a
slighter experience and less permanent values
than the melodies of Mozart. And intellect
comes into art because it comes into all experience and so into all values. The artist
with a profound intelligence sets himself a

harder problem, because his experience and his
values are more profound; and he uses his
intellect also in the solution of that problem.
He has a larger content to express; and the
object in which he expresses it is therefore
more complex and more highly organized.

Let us now apply these principles to drama.
Drama, of course, is capable of a direct statement of values; but such a statement will not
make a drama any more than it will make a
piece of music or a picture. Drama, like music
or pictures, is the object in which values are
communicated, and any statement of values is
irrelevant to it, unless that statement is what
a person of the drama would naturally say in
the circumstances; in which case it is there,
not as a statement of values, but as a part
of the drama. Hamlet does, now and again,
make a statement of his values which may
be also Shakespeare's; but, in so far as it is
relevant to the drama, it is there, not as a
statement of Shakespeare's values, but as what
Hamlet would say in those circumstances.
Hamlet is not Shakespeare's mouthpiece; he
is rather an embodiment of what Shakespeare
values; and the play is a success because

As an Æsthetic Document

Shakespeare, by the manner in which he presents Hamlet to us, makes us share his feelings for Hamlet. I speak in this case of Hamlet, the man, rather than of *Hamlet*, the play, because Hamlet, the man, is *Hamlet*, the play. Shakespeare seems in Hamlet, the man, to embody all that he himself most values in humanity. What he expresses is a very personal and individual value; and he does it through a very individual character. This does not mean, of course, that Shakespeare is preaching a sermon, that he is saying to us—" Here is my ideal man; let him also be yours." The artist, like the lover, has no propagandist purpose; but the mere fact that he values a certain kind of human being intensely causes him to express that value. And we see the intensity of Shakespeare's value for one kind of human being in the peculiar construction of *Hamlet*; it is what has caused him to make one character so predominant in it, to make the play itself, not a conflict of persons, but a conflict within the mind of Hamlet. The King and all the other persons of the play are almost passive spectators of the drama of Hamlet's mind, which they cannot understand.

What they do has dramatic value because of its effect on that drama rather than on the plot of the play. For instance, when the King tells Hamlet that he is to go to England, the interest lies in the manner in which Hamlet accepts the news, not in the news itself. In fact, all the other characters are seen through his eyes, in terms of his feelings. But the play succeeds because Hamlet is so interesting and attractive to us that, throughout, we wish to know, what Shakespeare wishes to tell us, namely, what is happening in Hamlet's mind.

And now I can answer, perhaps, that question—How is beauty achieved, where we should not expect it to be achieved, namely through a drama made out of the mental disorder of the hero?

Hamlet is a tragedy, and is beautiful, because of the intensity of value which is expressed in Hamlet himself. There would be no tragedy, and no beauty, if the jangled bells were not sweet, if the reason were not noble, and even sovereign, through all its disorder. That disorder, happening to a common mind or to a mind not valued by the author, might make a story pathologically interesting, it would not make a great work of art. That "unmistakable tone" which Mr. Eliot finds in *Hamlet* the play, comes from Hamlet himself and is the beauty of his character, which seems to flow out of it and to fill the whole play, seems indeed to be heightened by all contrasting characters. In fact, in *Hamlet*, values are expressed more completely through the presentment of a living man, than in any other play known to us; and that is the secret of its success and also of the many questions asked about it. Shakespeare has always troubled the critics, because he is so thoroughly and so merely the artist; his expression of his values is more embodied than the expression of any other dramatist. Thus, if we ask like Mr. Eliot, or like the Senior Wrangler about *Paradise Lost*, what *Hamlet* proves, there is no answer. It proves nothing, even about human nature; it *is* human nature. Aristotle or anyone else, if given the plot in a bare outline, might have doubted whether it could be related to any character; but Shakespeare has not merely related it to a character, he has made it the expression of a character; and that

G 97

is what puzzles the people who talk about plots by themselves or about psychology by itself. They have forgotten Hamlet himself, who compels us to believe in him and in all the events through which he lives and moves and has his being.

And in *Hamlet* more clearly than in any other play, we can see the justification of tragedy; which is that values can be more fully expressed in it than in comedy. Hamlet himself might be a character of comedy, a Mercutio, almost a melancholy Jacques; but, if he were, we should know and feel far less about him. Even Mercutio is most fully revealed to us, and is most valued by us, in his jests when he is dying; for then we see that his jesting is a part of himself, a reaction both trained and instinctive, and not mere high spirits or ingenuity or ambition of wit. And Hamlet, throughout, is like a man who jests dying; he does not put on an antic disposition but actually expresses suffering in terms of laughter; and this we should not know without his misfortune. It is no wonder that Shakespeare, the artist, should so have valued one who remains himself an artist even through mental disorder, and is even more of an artist because of it. Hamlet is never, even in the midst of horror, one who must tread a careful and narrow way so that he may not offend. He goes through life with a beautiful wilfulness, dancing rather than trudging; he can relish all kinds of experience, even the disorder of his own mind, because he can express them all. His very talk is a kind of dancing rather than our usual hand-to-mouth jog-trot of words. It reveals an extreme resilience of mind, which instantly transforms whatever happens into a finer expression of itself, with a personal comment always implied or expressed. Compared with other men, he is like a polished pebble by a dull one; all things are more clearly and more beautifully reflected in him.

To express such a character fully, it seems necessary that he should be subjected, not only to external, but to internal misfortune; or rather that external misfortune, of the kind to which he is subjected, must produce mental disorder. Hamlet would not be Hamlet if he dealt with the situation as Othello would deal with it; but, if he is to deal with it in his own way, we must have his mental disorder exposed to us. Therefore, if such a character as Hamlet is to be tragically treated—and only, if he is tragically, can he be fully treated —he must be treated in Shakespeare's manner. Mr. Eliot and some other critics, I suppose, would say that it is impossible to treat him tragically; the answer is that Shakespeare has done it; and the proof is that he presents Hamlet to us, not only vividly, but always in terms of beauty.

We resent mental disorder in a work of art if it seems to be there only to make our flesh, or our spirit, creep, or if it is misplaced science. We do not resent it in *Hamlet* because it is the necessary result of events, and because Hamlet himself is more clearly revealed to us by means of it. He is never "a case," but always himself; his range of mind, his quickness of transforming comment, are exhibited through his disorder as they could not be otherwise. For the very point of the play, that which interests us and moves us so profoundly, is the fact that he maintains all his graces, even his dancing speech, where other men would be either broken into silence or turned into mere instruments of revenge. He is neither narrowed nor made dumb, but remains more than ever Hamlet. Take, for instance, his courteous welcome to the players. How much more moving this is in its context, uttered by a man doomed and conscious of his doom, than it would be in a comedy. Or the scene with the recorders. There Hamlet is fantastic; but his fantasy is a triumph of his spirit, his sovereign reason even, over the situation and its effect upon his own mind. " 'Tis as easy as lying," he says to Guildenstern; a sentence of comedy implying that for Guildenstern lying is very easy; but Hamlet is triumphant because he can treat a tragic situation as if it were comedy; righteous indignation to Guildenstern would not be half so deadly, or so like Hamlet. And the relation between them enthrals us because it is tragic in a comic guise. Hamlet had made a serious appeal to Guildenstern, but now he knows it was vain; there is nothing in common between them, and he can comment on that fact only comically. It is however the peculiarity and the triumph of Hamlet, the artist, through all actual calamity, even through his own mental disorder, that he comments always with a bewildering, unexpected, rightness. If we saw him only in comedy, he would be for us undeveloped, like a charming youth who has never been tested in action. But he is tested and keeps his charm even when his behaviour is most outrageous; a proof that in that behaviour his character is revealed. In fact the unity of the play, and that inevitability without which a plot is mere machinery, is made by his character; and we must never criticize the plot without remembering this.

There has been much discussion in the past about the mixture of comedy and tragedy in the Elizabethan drama. It shocked Voltaire, who kept all his sense of propriety for the arts; and certainly, in the plays of Fletcher and lesser men, comedy is sometimes a mere diversion in tragedy and seems to be introduced because the dramatist is not sure that he can keep his audience quiet unless he gives them something to laugh at. But the mixture is justified in *Hamlet* where comedy and tragedy are fused, not only in the play, but in Hamlet himself. He could not be in the solemn

As an Æsthetic Document

French tragedy; but his drama is more tragic because of the fusion. Hamlet plays for himself the part of Mercutio and maintains it, almost to the end, in the scene with Osric.

Aristotle said that tragedy is more universal than history; and that is true if it means that values can be more directly expressed in it than in history. The historian is concerned rather with telling the truth about matters of fact than with the expression of values; it is a point of honour with him, or should be, not to adapt events or characters to the expression of values. His people are what they are, and he can only comment on the facts which are given to him. But to the dramatist no facts are given, even if he is dealing with history or revising an old play; and he can never defend a failure in the expression of values by saying that he is tied by his material, as the historian can never defend a failure to tell the truth by saying that he has expressed his values. So, if Shakespeare was indeed tied by his material and compelled to write as he would not otherwise have written, he has been particular like a historian where, as a dramatist, he should have béen universal. But the fact that he has so fully expressed his values in *Hamlet* proves that, whatever use he made of the old play, he was not tied to his material, that he wrote as a dramatist, not as a historian.

Unfortunately the saying of Aristotle that tragedy must be universal has been an obstruction both to the experience of dramatic art and to the production of it; for it has made both playwrights and critics forget that a certain kind of particularity is the essence of tragedy, since it becomes real, and so moving, only as its characters are real. One may say indeed that, while in comedy characters may be generic, in tragedy they must be specific. Racine moves us most when his characters are specific, are individuals, in spite of his generalized manner of writing; his peculiar power is to reveal individuals through this generalized speech. But there is nothing generalized in the speech of Hamlet, where it is most moving, most tragic even. He does at times talk Elizabethan rhetoric, as in the scene with his mother, especially in the first part of the speech—" Look here, upon this picture, and on this." But elsewhere he has a peculiar style, as he has a peculiar character, of his own.

> Sure, he that made us with such large discourse
> Looking before and after, gave us not
> That capability and god-like reason
> To fust in us unused. Now, whether it be
> Bestial oblivion, or some craven scruple
> Of thinking too precisely on the event,—
> A thought which, quartered, hath but one part
>   wisdom
> And ever three parts coward,—I do not know
> Why yet I live to say, "This thing's to do,"
> Sith I have cause, and will, and strength, and
>   means,
> To do't.

In that we seem to hear the very voice of Hamlet; and, I think, Shakespeare made a great advance in this play in the development of his blank verse because he was trying to express the particularity of Hamlet, to put into poetry his changes of mood, his vividness, his caprice, all that another writer would have left to prose. He has, both in style and in conception, poetized here a richer and more diverse content than had ever been poetized in the drama before; and the very capacities of blank verse and of the English language were enlarged by his success. But he made a

yet greater advance. The place of *Hamlet* in
the series of Shakespeare's plays is not certain.
Mr. E. K. Chambers, in his conjectured
chronology of the plays in the *Encyclopœdia
Britannica,* gives it to the year 1601 with
Twelfth Night, placing it two years after *Julius
Cœsar,* a year before *Troilus and Cressida,*
and two years before *Othello* and *Measure for
Measure.* It is, by general consent, the first of
the four great tragedies, and so the first of
those plays which place Shakespeare among
the chief poets of the world. Reading it after
the comedies, or *Henry IV.* and *Henry V.,* or
even *Julius Cœsar,* we are aware of a change
in Shakespeare's mind more easily noticed than
described. Before this change he had aimed
at dramatic success and achieved it, often by
the easiest way. The play had been the thing
for him always, something outside himself
which he had to make, as a craftsman makes
an object of use. And in making his plays, in
drawing his characters, he had, in the main,
accepted the standards of the world, not
obsequiously, but a little thoughtlessly, as if
he were too much occupied with the task of
making his plays to ask how he himself valued

the characters in them. It was enough for him to draw those characters as Titian drew his figures in a great sacred composition, magnificently but not very intimately, and with an eye to the composition itself more than to the individuals composing it. There are, of course, exceptions from the first, characters who seem to be there because he himself is interested in them. There is Berowne in *Love's Labour's Lost*, Mercutio in *Romeo and Juliet*; Richard II., an artist himself and a mouthpiece for poetry which runs away with the play; the melancholy of Antonio in the *Merchant of Venice*; Falstaff, a mouthpiece of humour which overpowers everything; Beatrice, who is too much alive compared with every one else in *Much Ado* except Benedick; and Brutus, who seems to be doubtfully drawn as if Shakespeare himself doubted what kind of man he was. Some of these seem to be drawn from real men or women; but there is not one of them, not even Richard II., who compels the play to be what it is. But in *Hamlet* Shakespeare set himself a different task and wrote with a different kind of interest. It is not the play, as a composition, that concerns him, but one particular man, as he is affected by the events and the other characters of the play. It is not that he has tried to draw an ideal character; if he had done that he would have yawned over the task; nor is it that he makes of Hamlet his own mouthpiece, though he does that sometimes. Hamlet is not drawn from himself, though we may be sure that he could not have drawn Hamlet's disorder except from some mental experience of his own. But Hamlet has come to life for him as no character had ever come to life before in any drama whatever; there is in him a peculiarity of values never before attempted. Hamlet himself means to us a certain way of feeling, thinking, and acting, of which the world had not before been aware and which it has valued ever since. You may say indeed that every man, at least of a certain order of mind, is Hamlet to himself; and that, not merely so that he may excuse to himself his own irresolutions, but because what we value in Hamlet is, not his actions, but his attitude to life. The hero is commonly the man who does things, and the things he means to do; but most of us secretly resent his glorification, as in Henry V., because we feel that, in real life, he is rewarded for a simplicity that comes often of lack of experiencing power.

But, in Hamlet, what Shakespeare values and makes us value is an extreme of experiencing power which, while it may produce the symptoms of irresolution, is not irresolution. In Hamlet there is neither uncertainty nor poverty of values; it is because his values are so rich and strong that he experiences all things so fully; and because he experiences them fully, he is more hurt by the calamity that befalls him than the common hero would be. But his hurt also is of a peculiar kind; the very calamity, beginning as external, becomes internal; his mind cannot adjust itself to the world of the court, as he finds it, or to life itself, since the world of the court is part of life. It is not merely conscience but his sovereign reason that rebels and is shaken by its own rebellion. The common hero, in such a case, would do something more effective; in a tragedy he would be killed doing it, and the tragedy would consist of his death. But Hamlet's tragedy is his life after he has learned the truth from the Ghost; and it consists in the fact that, by his very virtues, moral, intellectual and æsthetic, he is prevented from doing anything effective. It is the tragedy of " Captive good attending captain ill "; and yet we are sure that this very capacity for suffering is more to be valued than the common hero's effectiveness. We may not be able to say why; we may, when the spell of Hamlet is no longer upon us, even ask why he does not act like the common hero; but, so long as we are under his spell, we do value him, not in terms of what he does, but in terms of himself.

In *Hamlet* there is the first vivid and complete representation of a kind of character which still bewilders and fascinates us, the character, namely, which possesses, and expresses itself in terms of, an incessant double consciousness. Hamlet is one of those who are aware, not only of the desires, purposes, pleasures, and pains of the moment, but also of their own permanent attitude to all things, and of a general situation, not only of themselves but even of the universe. It is not that he is a professed philosopher or critic, but that his mind works, not like the minds of most men in unison, but in harmony and so, sometimes, in discord. All his thoughts, feelings, words, actions even, are richer than those of other men because of the accompaniment supplied by his permanent attitude, and the implied comment of that attitude on all that happens to him. Such men fascinate us by a superior disinterestedness, intellectual rather than moral; they seem to be not merely themselves, but a larger intellectual conscience contemplating themselves and all things. They are commonest in the most civilized societies, impossible perhaps among savages, and rare in simple, impulsive ages like the Elizabethan; but always, when they appear and play a part in history, they arouse a peculiar interest even in those who least understand them. Julius Cæsar seems to have been such a man; and that is why he interests us so much more than other able men of action, such as Cromwell or Napoleon, with only a single consciousness; and why Shakespeare's Cæsar, who has no double consciousness, disappoints us. Another example, nearer to our own time, is Disraeli, and we forgive in him what we would not forgive in the single consciousness of Gladstone.

We may be puzzled by the value we put

upon this double consciousness, but it is to us a prophecy of a higher state of being, of men who shall escape permanently from the narrowing tyranny of the struggle for life, who shall be artists and philosophers even while engaged in that struggle, concerned not only to succeed in this or that but at the same time to live a continuous life of thought and expression. We value such a man above, even, specialized artists or philosophers, who may be beings of simple consciousness, because he is what they do, and does, however imperfectly, achieve that fusion of the æsthetic and intellectual with the practical which is the lasting ideal of the human mind. The greatest example of this fusion known to us in history is Christ, and, in literature, Hamlet; and we have the same deep, if bewildered, interest in both. We feel about both—that they understand; and so Shakespeare himself, in *Hamlet*, becomes for us the poet who understands, not merely the great but specialized artist of the earlier plays. He is also, of course, a greater artist because, possessed by his own passionate value for this kind of character whom he has introduced into art, he has been able to devise a drama, unlike

any former drama, which will express that
character in all its unity and diversity. The
very discord of the double consciousness, caused
by Hamlet's calamity, reveals, as nothing else
could, its underlying and implied harmony.
There is still the permanent attitude, the
passionate disinterestedness, maintained in the
face of a hideous, pressing, duty; the fusion of
the intellectual and the æsthetic with the
practical, even when the practical is so fatally
in conflict with them. And the tragedy of
Hamlet, a tragedy possible only to the double
consciousness, consists in this conflict between
the permanent attitude and the practical task,
and in the vain effort to recover that harmony
which, to such minds, is a necessity of life.
"Thou wouldst not think how ill all's here
about my heart"—Hamlet says just before the
end; and Horatio advises—"If your mind
dislike anything, obey it"; he does not understand that Hamlet's mind is not at odds with
any particular thing, that he is commenting,
not on a task of the moment, but on a
permanent condition, which can be ended only
by death.

To judge such a tragedy by tragedies of

external circumstance, to expect to understand Hamlet's motives as easily as those of Othello or Coriolanus, is to misunderstand. It is nearer to the tragedy of Macbeth than to any other, because Macbeth is forced, by a crime far below the level of his character, into a conflict between himself and all his immodest tasks, and so into a permanent condition that can be ended only by death. But in Macbeth the double consciousness, what there is of it, is evoked by his crime and the discord of his nature which it causes. In Hamlet it is there always, and we become more and more aware of it, in all its beauty and subtlety, with every event of the play.

So the play does for us, in an extreme degree, what it is the function of all art to do for us. It gives us the sense of values apart from all consequences, all practical issues, as that sense is given to us by a great tune. In that consists the liberating power of art; it makes for us a kind of experience in which we do not need to look before or after, in which what *is* is also expressed, and so directly, that we can value it directly. Hamlet, expressed for us by Shakespeare, is charged for us with

As an Æsthetic Document

Shakespeare's values. They ring in his speech, and the emotion of the creator sounds in the music of the creature, so that often the play seems to escape from itself and to become a hymn of the beauty of the human mind triumphing over all odds.

In one place Hamlet is his own chorus and seems prophetic of his commentators—

> Why, look you now, how unworthy a thing you make of me! You would play upon me; you would seem to know my stops; you would pluck out the heart of my mystery; you would sound me from the lowest note to the top of my compass; and there is much music, excellent voice in this little organ, yet cannot you make it speak. 'Sblood, do you think I am easier to be played on than a pipe? Call me what instrument you will, though you can fret me, you cannot play upon me.

There remains a mystery after all that we can say; but we shall not pluck out its heart by trying to prove that it is no mystery. As Mr. Robertson says: " You cannot make a silk purse out of a sow's ear "; and not even Shakespeare could have made Hamlet out of a play of Kyd's.

APPENDIX

Did Hamlet delay to kill the King? ‿

EVEN the fact of delay has been denied. Mr. Robertson, after speaking of "the singular unanimity, preserved down to our own day, with which the critics of all schools have taken for granted that Hamlet does in a remarkable way delay his revenge," continues thus—"All the while, unless we decide that Hamlet's duty, after hearing the Ghost's tale, is to proceed instantly to slay the King, there has been as little delay as may well be. It is solely as regards the interval between Acts I. and II. that a charge can be laid. . . . But it is not upon this interval, or upon Hamlet's quiescence therein, that the stress of criticism has fallen." But he adds, with his usual fairness—"One thing must be said for the critics. Shakespeare himself has in a manner given them their warrant, by the two vivid soliloquies in which he makes Hamlet impeach himself." He then proceeds to explain this

117

impeachment away as being partly the result of a cue from the old play—(which does not survive)—and partly of Shakespeare's own idiosyncrasy of idealistic disregard of time. This explanation I do not understand.

But an American critic, Professor Stoll (in his *Hamlet: an Historical and Comparative Study*, published by the University of Minnesota), maintains that Hamlet does not seriously impeach himself. His object is to prove that Hamlet is not an unusual or novel character at all, but the typical hero of a typical revenge play, very like Hieronimo in *The Spanish Tragedy*. In such plays, he says, the hero reproaches himself for delay, and others reproach him, to keep up the interest of the story. "As a motive or link in a story the device, though a makeshift, is not uncommon." Professor Stoll quotes the lines—

> Now, whether it be
> Bestial oblivion, or some craven scruple
> Of thinking too precisely on the event,—
> A thought which, quartered, hath but one part
>   wisdom
> And ever three parts coward,—I do not know
> Why yet I live to say, "This thing's to do,"
> Sith I have cause, and will, and strength, and means,
> To do't.

And then proceeds with these astonishing remarks: "Here again the charge is unmade in the making. Here, though there is more analysis, Hamlet himself accepts none of the alternatives that offer. He 'does not know'; he has 'will and strength and means to do it.' These are the last words, and it is they that stick in our minds. Shakespeare will not suffer him after all, to testify against himself. What he does is to let Hamlet pull himself together."

But the "last words," quoted by Professor Stoll are not the last words of the soliloquy. Hamlet is preaching resolution to himself, as elsewhere. He rambles on and on, in a manner peculiar to himself among Shakespeare's characters, and a few lines further on asks himself—

> How stand I then,
> That have a father killed, a mother stained,
> Excitements of my reason and my blood,
> And let all sleep?

And he may well ask; for, after the play-scene has made him certain of the King's crime, he is on his way to England with Rosencrantz and Guildenstern. It is that fact which causes him, in this soliloquy, to contrast himself with Fortinbras, and to cry—

> How all occasions do inform against me.

If Shakespeare here is "letting Hamlet pull himself together," that is what he is doing throughout the play; and at the end of it

Hamlet does not pull himself together but is forced to act. He kills the King only because the King has contrived his own death.

It is no wonder that Mr. Eliot, after reading Mr. Robertson and Professor Stoll, and accepting their view, calls the play a failure. If Professor Stoll is right, it is one, and all the interest which generations have found in it, and in the character of Hamlet, is based upon a misunderstanding. Hamlet is a perfectly straightforward hero, or ruffian, of a melodrama, who talks to prolong it, saying what neither he nor his creator means, because that is the manner in which such plays are prolonged.

But now consider the facts. After the first Act we should expect the theme of Hamlet's revenge, so clearly stated, to be in the foreground. But what happens? In the second Act, for some time, Hamlet does not appear at all; there is only talk of his strange behaviour, which, if it has any dramatic purpose at all, must be meant to heighten our expectation of that behaviour. Then, at last, Hamlet appears "reading," and behaves strangely to Polonius. There follows the interview with Rosencrantz and Guildenstern, and then the interview with the Players; and still there is no hint of revenge. But the moment Hamlet is alone,

Appendix

at the very end of the Act, he falls to reproaching himself for his delay with the words—"Now I am alone."

It would be impossible to insist upon the fact of the delay more strongly, or upon Hamlet's strange state of mind. But even then he is reminded of his duty by the artistic emotion of the Player; and he hits upon the device of the play so that he may convince himself that the Ghost was not a devil come to abuse him. Mr. Robertson says that the critics have not insisted upon the delay between Acts I. and II. (which appears to have been about two months); but Hamlet insists upon it and reproaches himself with frenzy. Professor Stoll quotes the words—

Who calls me villain? breaks my pate across?
Plucks off my beard, and blows it in my face?
Tweaks me by the nose? gives me the lie i' the
    throat,
As deep as to the lungs? Who does me this?

and then remarks, " Echo answers—Who? and he rouses himself and shakes off the slanders he has been showering upon himself, like the true and sensible man that he is." But does he? The soliloquy continues—

Swounds, I should take it; for it cannot be
But I am pigeon-liver'd and lack gall
To make oppression bitter.

Then he falls to abusing the King, and,
finally, compares himself to a whore that un-
packs her heart with words. I am tempted
to wonder about Professor Stoll, as about Mr.
Eliot, whether he has read the play on which
he comments so strangely.

Act III. begins again with wonder about
Hamlet's state of mind. There follows the
play-scene; Hamlet's refusal to kill the King
at his prayers; the interview with his mother;
the death of Polonius, which certainly proves
that Hamlet has no scruples about killing the
King; the appearance of the Ghost, who
speaks of his almost blunted purpose; his
dispatch to England by the King's orders;
and the soliloquy on the way, in which he
contrasts himself with Fortinbras. When Mr.
Robertson says that a charge of delay can
be laid solely as regards the interval between
Acts I. and II., he must forget this journey
to England. Professor Stoll does not forget
it but maintains that Hamlet " is in custody,
and a man is not considered feeble or incapable
because he does not fight the police when
arrested." But the play itself says nothing of
this; indeed elsewhere Professor Stoll himself
remarks—" The King fears him, and shrinks
from bringing him to account for Polonius'
death." In the play, the King tells Hamlet

that he must go to England for his special safety and Hamlet instantly answers—" Good," in spite of the fact that thereby he is indefinitely delaying his revenge. Twice he says " Come, for England!" and departs gaily with those words, leaving the King safe on his throne; while the King, so far from using or threatening force, says to Rosencrantz and Guildenstern — " Tempt him with speed aboard." Shakespeare, even if he was writing a commonplace melodrama, was not utterly incompetent at that. If he had meant us to believe that Hamlet went to England because he was forced and in custody, he would have made that fact, and not the contrary, appear in the behaviour of Hamlet and the King. Nor would he have made Hamlet himself insist, in the next scene, that he had strength and means to take his revenge (which would have been untrue if he was in custody), but that he was failing to take it through his own fault.

Then Professor Stoll, dropping the custody theory, says that Hamlet falls in with his deportation as part of his plan. Hardly as part of his plan to kill the King! And he maintains that, after the soliloquy, " How all occasions do inform against me "—" the neglect and delay are over and done with." But are they? When Hamlet appears again in the

Grave-digger's scene in Act V., he says nothing of his revenge, but discourses at length about death and dissolution—a discourse which is only cut short by the appearance of the King with Ophelia's funeral. Here, as elsewhere, it needs an external reminder to recall him to his revenge. Then, in Scene II., he is again maintaining to Horatio that he has a right to kill the King, arguing all over again the same old question. To which the practical Horatio replies—

> It must be shortly known to him from England,
> What is the issue of the business there—

meaning that Hamlet must be quick about it. To this Hamlet replies that he will be quick about it—

> It will be short ; the interim is mine—

and then falls, with his usual irrelevance, to regretting his treatment of Laertes. Then follows the interview with Osric in which Hamlet again forgets everything in his ridicule of Osric; then the short scene in which he expresses his foreboding of the end; and then the end with a rush.

I have spoken of Hamlet's irrelevance; and this is more obvious, more insisted upon by Shakespeare, than his delay. All the brilliance and subtlety of his character are

Appendix

shown in that irrelevance; but, if it is insisted upon merely to prolong the action and because it is proper to the hero of a revenge play, then indeed the world has been mistaken about *Hamlet*. My answer to those, if there are any besides Mr. Eliot, who are convinced by Professor Stoll, is — Read *The Spanish Tragedy*. If then they think that *Hamlet* is a play of the same kind, with the same devices and motives, there is no more to be said. But since few readers, I think, are likely to be convinced by Professor Stoll, I have dealt with his theory in an appendix.

THE PROBLEM

OF

"HAMLET"

BY

J. M. ROBERTSON

Author of "Shakespeare and Chapman,"
"The Baconian Heresy," etc.

LONDON: GEORGE ALLEN & UNWIN LTD
RUSKIN HOUSE, 40 MUSEUM STREET, W.C. 1

First published in 1919

PREFACE

FOR some years, as a result of a lifetime rather largely devoted to Shakespeare study, the author has been engaged on a work on " The Canon of Shakespeare," designed to deal with all the problems coming under that title. In 1905 he preluded the undertaking with a volume entitled " Did Shakespeare write TITUS ANDRONICUS ? " which, rewritten and greatly expanded, he hopes shortly to reissue as a practical introduction to the study of the entire " Canon." The whole ground, it is hoped, need not be covered on the same scale ; and a number of the more problematic plays have been dealt with in sections of moderate length. The complete work, however—if the author should live to complete it—will inevitably be a bulky one ; and he hopes, before putting it in a final form, to have the benefit of expert criticism of at least a number of the sections.

It is proposed, accordingly, to issue some of them separately. This course has already been begun by the publication of the volume SHAKESPEARE AND CHAPMAN (1917), which sets forth the most revolutionary of the critical inferences to which the author has thus far been led, and which involves a fresh consideration of the origins of a number of the Plays. One of those there referred to has since been fully discussed in the paper on " The Problem of THE MERRY WIVES OF WINDSOR," published for the Shakespeare Association (Chatto & Windus). The present volume, which reviews and attempts to resolve the most interesting and the most extensive debate relating to any of them, is submitted as an illustration of what is claimed to be the proper method of investigating all, for the given purpose.

Only since my MS. was put in the hands of the printer have I received Mr. J. Dover Wilson's interesting and valuable contributions to the inquiry entitled " The Copy for ' Hamlet,' 1603, and the ' Hamlet ' Transcript, 1593 " (A. Moring, Ltd., 1918). Coinciding, I think, in the main with my view, that investigation opens up several correlative questions ; and I have thought it well to await the further inquiry promised by Mr. Wilson before attempting to connect his results with mine.

March 1919.

CONTENTS

THE PROBLEM OF "HAMLET"

I

THE ÆSTHETIC PROBLEM

§ 1. Subjective Theories.

THERE is no better illustration of the need for a study of the genesis of the Shakespeare Plays than the endless discussion of the æsthetic problem of HAMLET. It has continued for two centuries, latterly with the constant preoccupation of finding a formula which shall reduce the play to æsthetic consistency; and every solution in turn does but ignore some of the data which motived the others. All alike are inconclusive, because all ignore in effect, even when they make mention of it, the essential fact that Shakespeare's HAMLET is an adaptation of an older play, which laid down the main action, embodying a counter-sense which the adaptation could not transmute. To constate the successive theses is to make this clear.

The formula put by Goethe in WILHELM MEISTER'S LEHRJAHRE—that the tragedy is one of an overwhelming task laid upon a spirit incapable of it [1]—is, to begin

---

[1] " To me it is clear that Shakespeare meant to present a great deed laid upon a soul that is not capable of it. . . . Here is an oak-tree planted in a costly vase that should have nurtured only lovely flowers : the roots expand ; the vase is shattered."—*Lehrjahre*, B. iv, Cap. xiii, end. Cp. Cap. iii.

with, an imperfect substitute for that put by Henry Mackenzie in his essay in the Edinburgh MIRROR (No. 99) in 1780.[1] Already in Mackenzie's day it was common ground that " Of all the characters of Shakespeare, that of Hamlet has been generally thought the most difficult to be reduced to any fixed or settled principle " ; and Mackenzie set himself " to inquire whether any leading idea can be found, upon which these apparent contradictions may be reconciled." He found it in " an extreme sensibility of mind, apt to be strongly impressed by its situation, and overpowered by the feelings which that situation excites." The terrible circumstances unhinged those " principles of action which in a happier situation would have yielded a happy life." Hamlet's character is thus " often variable and uncertain," and the suggestion is offered that " this is the very character which Shakespeare meant to allot to him." " Finding such a character in real life, of a person endowed with feelings so delicate as to border on weakness, with sensibility too exquisite to allow of determined action," he " has placed it where it could be best exhibited, in scenes of wonder, of terror, of imagination."

This " subjective " theorem, which best of all provides for the various contingencies, anticipates and transcends both that of Goethe,[2] which might be the formula of a hundred tragedies, and that of Schlegel and Coleridge—

[1] Professor Herford, in his paper on " Recent Contributions to Shakespeare Criticism " in the *Book of Homage* (p. 182), while noting that Goethe's criticism is misleading and in some of its implications quite wrong, pronounces that it " virtually started the Hamlet problem." This, as we shall see, holds only for Goethe's own age. The discussion goes back to Gildon at least.

[2] As Hermann Türck remarks (*Das psychologische Problem in der Hamlet-Tragödie*, 1894, p. 8), Goethe's view of Hamlet is an account of his own Werther, whom Türck describes almost in Mackenzie's formula as a nature " yielding to every impression."

that Hamlet is the victim of an excess of the reflective faculty, which unfits him for action. The answer to both of these was given in 1828 by Coleridge's son Hartley,[1] who pointed out that "feebleness of mind, the fragility of a china vase, lack of power and energy, are not the characteristics of Hamlet. So far from it, he is represented as fearless, almost above the strength of humanity. He does not ' set his life at a pin's fee'." Hartley in turn proffered the formula that "it is not the weight and magnitude, the danger and difficulty of the deed imposed as a duty, that weighs upon his soul and enervates the sinews of his moral being, but the preternatural contradiction involved in the duty itself, the irregular means through which the duty is promulgated and known." In short, Shakespeare's purpose was " to show the evil and confusion which must be introduced into the moral world by a sensible communication between natural and supernatural beings."[2]

This thesis, which is confuted by the TEMPEST and the DREAM, has never made any avowed converts; but the denial of Hamlet's alleged weakness of nature has often been repeated, and must many times have been made by independent English students before and after Hartley Coleridge, as it was by Ulrici (as he supposed, for the first time) in 1839, and after him by many other Germans,[3] down to our own day. Nevertheless, the

---

[1] In the essay On the Character of Hamlet, in Blackwood's Magazine, reprinted in Essays and Marginalia, 1851, i. 151 sq.

[2] Essay on Shakespeare a Tory and a Gentleman, vol. cited, p. 144.

[3] See his Shakespeare's Dramatic Art, Eng. trans. 1876, i. 483, note. Goethe's thesis is now almost universally given up. Gervinus, however, in 1850 could still write : " Since this riddle has been solved by Goethe in his Wilhelm Meister, it is scarcely to be conceived that it ever was one."—Shakespeare Commentaries, Eng. trans. i. 109.

kindred doctrine that Hamlet delayed his action because
he could not make up his mind has continued to appear
in critical literature, and still has many adherents.
Lowell, taking it over from Coleridge, held it as a fixed
dogma, and imposed it in his eloquent essay SHAKESPEARE
ONCE MORE, in some respects the most influential study
of Shakespeare in its generation.   Lowell alludes to the
old story from which the play derives, and he must have
known that the critics inferred a pre-Shakespearean
play ; but he confidently proceeds on the assumption
that Shakespeare's conception of Hamlet's character
" was the ovum out of which the whole organism was
hatched," finding even that " Hamlet seems the natural
result of the mixture of the father and mother in this
temperament, the resolution and persistence of the one,
like sound timber worm-holed and made shaky, as it
were, by the other's infirmity of will and discontinuity
of purpose."

Thus is assigned to the victim of heredity both resolution and irresolution ; while the " temperament,"
with an " imagination in overplus " that has no heredity,
determines the action all the same.   Hamlet, accordingly, is duly scolded through many pages, with no
attempt to face either conflicting data or conflicting
theories.   So strange an anomaly as the occurrence of
the " To be " soliloquy after the ghost scene is merely
turned to the account of the indictment : " He doubts
the immortality of the soul after seeing his father's
spirit "—a flat misrepresentation.   What Hamlet does
is to say that " no traveller returns "—which constitutes
an anomaly in the construction of the play, not in Hamlet's
" character."

ll the while, Lowell does not believe that Shakespeare

wrote this or any of his plays with a "didactic purpose." The implication would seem to be that the dramatist left that to his readers, simply providing a hero who could be scolded, as never was hero before, by literary persons conscious of their own consummate fitness for killing a guilty uncle at a moment's notice. "If we must draw a moral from Hamlet," writes Lowell, "it would seem to be that Will is Fate, and that, Will once abdicating, the inevitable successor is the regency of Chance. Had Hamlet acted instead of musing how good it would be to act, the king might have been the only victim. As it is, all the main actors in the story are the fortuitous sacrifice of his irresolution." With a fine unconsciousness, the critic has previously observed : "With what perfect tact and judgment Shakespeare, in the advice to the players, makes him an exquisite critic!" And yet subsequent exquisite critics, as we see, are quite confident that they have escaped the "great vice of character" they assign to Shakespeare's prince. No one thinks it necessary to vituperate Macbeth for slaying Duncan, or Othello for murdering Desdemona ; still less is Desdemona denounced for prevaricating about her handkerchief and thereby entailing her own and Othello's death ; but for *not* killing Claudius either at the start or in the praying scene, Hamlet has been the theme of a hundred denunciations by zealous moralists. It would be odd if Shakespeare, who, says Lowell, "never acted without unerring judgment," had deliberately planned for that.

At this point we may fitly pause to note the singular unanimity, preserved down to our own day, with which the critics of all schools have taken for granted that Hamlet *does* in a remarkable way delay his revenge. To judge

from their language, he procrastinates to a degree that
calls for an explanation ; and the burden of their testimony is either that no explanation is given or that it
lies in his character, temperament, or mood. And all
the while, unless we decide that Hamlet's duty, after
hearing the Ghost's tale, is to proceed *instantly* to slay
the king, there has been as little delay as might well
be ! It is solely as regards the interval between Acts I
and II that a charge can be laid. There has been time
for the journey of the ambassadors from Denmark to
Norway and back, and for Polonius to think of sending
Reynaldo to inquire about Laertes' doings in Paris.
But it is not upon this interval, or upon Hamlet's
quiescence therein, that the stress of criticism has fallen,
though it is only in this period, of which we see nothing,
that Hamlet can be said to have shown any sensitive
recoil from the act of vengeance. The latest critic to
revive that charge, Professor W. F. Trench, after sternly
censuring Hamlet for being " unable to decide upon a
course of action " and for " resolving to let himself go "
after the Ghost scene,[1] expressly pronounces [2] that
" at the end of Act II, Fate is still well disposed to
Hamlet." That is to say, there has been no deadly
delay up to the point at which Hamlet, retrospec-
tively hesitating to believe in the Ghost, plans the
court play.

On that view, the " procrastination " of Hamlet resolves itself into the single abstention from slaying the
king while he prays. Having made up his mind that
the hero's sole faculty is to talk and " preach," the critic
scornfully comments that when Hamlet resheathes his

---

[1] *Shakespeare's Hamlet : A New Commentary*, 1913, p. 87,
[2] *Id.* p. 127.

sword he has "caught sight of and grasped an excuse for procrastinating *once more*;" [1] which must mean either that Hamlet ought to have killed the king *at* the play a few minutes before, or that his previous delay had after all been unpardonable. At once we are moved to put the two questions whether king-killing is supposed to be usually accomplished with the extreme promptitude here insisted on; and whether any stage-character but Hamlet has ever been subjected to such a rigour of criticism. And if, further, we do but ask ourselves what kind of a moral and what kind of an æsthetic effect would have been secured by Hamlet's stabbing the king in the back while he knelt at prayer, we may be led to question yet further whether the moral efficiency of Hamlet is not after all rather higher than that of his censors.

Save for that one episode, wherein, whatever be supposed to be the real motive, procrastination is simple decency, the choice to kill manfully at another time rather than to stab in the back, there is no further "delay" on Hamlet's part, the action proceeding breathlessly up to his deportation, to be resumed on his return, whereafter he can be accused of procrastination only by those who argue that he ought at the very outset to have proved his manhood by raising the mob as did Laertes, the type of headlong precipitation. Considered from the standpoint of practical politics, even of assassination politics, Hamlet's "delay" is negligible; while his faculty for volition and action would seem to be sufficiently proved by his murderously prompt disposal of Polonius and the two courtiers, and his boarding of the pirate ship.

[1] *Id.* p. 171.

But one thing must be said for the critics. Shakespeare himself has in a manner given them their warrant, by the two vivid soliloquies in which he makes Hamlet impeach himself. And this the dramatist has done partly on a cue from the old play, partly in virtue of his own idiosyncrasy of idealistic disregard of time. Under circumstances which we shall discuss later, he took up the old play which he has transmuted, and finding in it an action that to his time-discounting sense was one of unexplained delay (being so felt by Hamlet himself on the second visitation of the Ghost in the old play), elaborated that aspect of the hero as he did every other. In all likelihood he was responding to an impression of the theatre which chimed with his idiosyncrasy—revealed in the impossible treatment of time in OTHELLO and MEASURE FOR MEASURE, to name no others.[1] That Hamlet " shilly-shallied " was in all likelihood the verdict of the audiences before the critics made it their theme ; because the " two hours' traffic of the stage " psychologically predisposes us to an exigence which in reading a novel we should not think of practising. So much must happen in so short a space that normal standards of criticism of conduct are cast aside ; and inasmuch as Shakespeare in his adaptation assented to this, treating Hamlet as one who inexplicably procrastinated, the litigation set up by the critics must be allowed to proceed. But, in the interest alike of Shakespeare and of critical science, it must be logically conducted to the end ; and this, as we have seen and shall see further, has not been

---

[1] Whether this telescoping of time is specially a result of the dramatist's adaptation of other men's work is a problem which calls for separate treatment. It has also to be asked whether the academic insistence on the " unities " moved him to evade the proper indications of time-interval.

done. What has been achieved is but a series of conflicting propositions, all professing to sum up the case without facing all the facts.

§ 2. Objective Theories.

After the rebuttal of the Goethean formula of temperamental incompetence,[1] the next step was to frame a formula of *objective* hindrances which delayed Hamlet's revenge. In 1845, George Fletcher, in an article in the WESTMINSTER REVIEW,[2] dwelt on the overpowering force of the obstacles; and made an allusion to the " preternatural embarrassment of the most horrible kind superadded," which points back to Hartley Coleridge. In 1846 J. L. Klein, the German historian of modern drama, set forth in the BERLINER MODENSPIEGEL the thesis that Hamlet was barred from action by the manner of the crime and the nature of his knowledge of it, which could not be offered as evidence to justify an assassination of the guilty king. Another German, Levinstein, is cited as putting the same view before Werder. Professor Karl Werder, in turn, independently framed and expounded the same thesis in his lectures on HAMLET at the Berlin University in 1859–60, and again in 1871–2.[3]

[1] Lowell, having plumped for the formula of Schlegel and Coleridge, naturally joined in deprecating that of Goethe, observing that he " seems to have considered the character too much from one side," but does not argue the point at all well. Hamlet, he remarks, " was hardly a sentimentalist " like Werther. On Goethe's side it might be replied that Lowell makes him very truly a sentimentalist, in that he lives in sentiment and is finally determined to action by " chance."

[2] Reprinted in *Studies of Shakespeare* in 1847. Furness does not note this essay in his Variorum edition; and Rolfe, who cites it in his 1903 ed. of *Hamlet* and in his introduction to Miss Wilder's translation of Werder (Putnams, 1907), does not mention Hartley Coleridge.

[3] Lectures published in full in the *Preussische Jahrbücher*, 1873–4, and reprinted in book form, 1875 and 1893.

Even as the champions of the subjective theory, impressed by the evidence of Hamlet's procrastination, ignored that of his faculty for prompt and vigorous action, so the champions of the objective theory, impressed by that evidence, dwelt on the insurmountable difficulties of Hamlet's task, and ignored his own self-accusations. Werder, whose prolix and declamatory handling of a fairly plausible thesis reveals its inadequacy to a considerate reader, seems to have made many converts, including Furness, Hudson, Corson and Rolfe,[1] all of whom, like him, took for granted the thoroughly planned character of the play, though they admitted minor perplexities. But it is precisely on the view of a thorough plan that their thesis most completely breaks down. If in Shakespeare's view Hamlet was faced by insuperable difficulties of circumstance, it was Shakespeare's plain business to let us see as much. And this he never once does. His Hamlet " does not know," any more than we, why his task recedes from him.

Surprisingly popular latterly in the United States, Werder's theory had small success among European critics, in Germany or elsewhere. It is marked by the " vigour and rigour " which Arnold ascribed to German theories in general, the tactic of driving the thesis anyhow through or over the facts which is so characteristic of German publicism—and politics. Of his own thesis Werder writes : " That this point for a century long should never have been seen is the most incomprehensible thing that has ever happened in æsthetic criticism from the very beginning of its existence "—a kind of vocifer-

---

[1] Mr. W. H. Widgery (*Harness Prize Essays on the First Quarto of 'Hamlet,'* 1880, p. 185 sq.) adopted the position.

ation that does not usually accompany real discoveries. The stress of Werder's case lies on the position that a mere killing of the king would not only put Hamlet himself in danger from the indignant people but would wholly fail to secure his real end—the *judicial* conviction and execution of the murderer. To the retort that Hamlet never once indicates any such ideal, Werder replies that the " state of the case " speaks for him ; and to the further retort that such an argument is merely a *petitio principii* his genial supporter, Mr. W. J. Rolfe, replies that the " subjective " theorists, who oppose, argue in the same fashion.[1] That is doubtless true ; but Werder's thesis is not thereby to be established.

Professor Tolman, who regretfully rejects Werder's solution, leaves it intact by merely countering with the subjective theory—" Character " as against " Fate." The complete or general answer to Werder is that not only is his explanation nowhere indicated in the play, not only is his conception of the need for a judicial punishment alien to the whole ethic and atmosphere of the play, but it comes to the same thing as the subjective theory in that it makes Hamlet recoil from the possible course and fasten on an impossible one. How should the king be convicted ? On his own evidence, under torture ? A public investigation is the last thing Hamlet could critically be supposed to wish ; and neither his pictured compatriots nor the Elizabethan audience can be conceived as craving for it. Above all, the audience. Yet Werder is as insistent for his arbitrary hypothesis as he is blind to the case for the subjective

---

[1] Introd. to *The Heart of Hamlet's Mystery* (trans. of Werder's lectures, 1907), p. 18.

theory. In the closet scene, he observes [1] " the Ghost says *only* :

> Do not forget. This visitation
> Is but to whet *thy almost blunted purpose*."

Only! We are apparently invited to suppose that the Ghost, like all the subjective critics, was mistaken! Rolfe, most lovable of Shakespeareans, actually meets Professor Bradley's challenge to face the text by saying that an external obstacle is " clearly implied " in Hamlet's

> Sith I have cause and will and strength and *means*
> To do't——

the very lines that are preceded by

> *I do not know*
> Why yet I live to say, ' This thing's to do.'

And against the challenge to explain away Hamlet's phrases about his " sword " and his " arm," Rolfe affirms that the words are used " *because* the *killing* of the king is the end or aim of his task," which must wait " until he can ' bring the king to *public justice.*' " It suffices to confront this, once more, with Hamlet's words in the praying scene :—

> Up, sword, and know thou a more horrid hent:
> *When he is drunk, asleep, or in his rage,*
> *Or in the incestuous pleasures of his bed ;*
> *At gaming, swearing, or about some act*
> *That has no relish of salvation in't ;*
> *Then trip him,* that his heels may kick at heaven . . .

---

[1] Trans. cited, p. 47.

Before this, the " public justice " theory simply disappears, even as does the subjective theory before the challenge of Hamlet's slaughterous acts, though that theory naturally fastens on the lines before us as indicating a recoil from the decisive action needed.

Well may Rolfe avow that " All the theories, whether subjective or objective, have their difficulties." [1] Those of the theory he embraces, however, are the most obvious and most instantly fatal of all. Framed and adopted because of the failure of the subjective theory in any of its forms to meet the data, it reveals itself as still worse founded than they ; and it accordingly makes by far the worse figure in debate. Admitted by its adherents to fail in meeting all the difficulties, and raising as it does new difficulties of the most hopeless kind, it compels us to seek sounder ground.

§ 3. Theory of Defect in the Dramatist.

Both the subjective and the objective explanations being so obviously inadequate to the data, the capable Gustav Rümelin (afterwards Kanzler of Tübingen) in his SHAKESPEARESTUDIEN, published in book form in 1866, countered the critics in general with a thesis of " faults of the poet " as against alike that of " faults of the hero " and the claim to justify the play as a whole. Bent on countering " Shakespeare-Mania " in the centenary year 1864, Rümelin was more concerned to impugn Shakespeare's work than to explain it ; and he in turn,

---

[1] Rolfe is quaintly at strife with his leader on one point. On the " times are out of joint " speech he writes (p. 37) : " Most significant words, though the critics have taken little note of them." In the same volume (p. 108) we find Werder writing : " Critics have made too much of these words."

though he pointed to the old Hamlet-saga as conditioning Shakespeare's play, did not substantiate his case by the data as to the pre-Shakespearean tragedy of Kyd. On the other hand, Hebler, who resisted alike Rümelin and Werder, continued to maintain a position [1] in which the dilemmas of the play were partly ignored.

Rümelin's position, as it happened, had long been anticipated by British common-sense. Gildon in 1710 had charged on the play " abundance of errors in the conduct and design," insisting that " Shakespeare was master of this story," and therefore responsible for the plot. Hanmer in 1730, in turn, pronounced that " our poet by keeping too close to the groundwork of his plot has fallen into an absurdity "; adding : " Had Hamlet gone naturally to work . . . there would have been an end of our play. The poet, therefore, was obliged to delay his hero's revenge ; but then he *should have contrived some good reason for it.*" [2]　And Mackenzie in 1780 confessed of the dramatist : " Of the structure of his stories, or the probability of his incidents, he is frequently careless "; and again : " It may perhaps be doing Shakespeare no injustice to suppose that he sometimes began a play without having fixed in his mind, in any determined manner, the plan or conduct of his piece."

The same caveat was otherwise put by Edgar Poe :

In all commentating upon Shakespeare there has been a radical error never yet mentioned. It is the error of attempting to expound

---

[1] *Aufsätze über Shakespeare,* 2te Aufl. 1872.

[2] Cited by Malone, Var. ed. at end of play. Professor Bradley has, I think, done Hanmer injustice (*Shakespearean Tragedy,* 2nd ed. p. 91) by not citing the last sentence. It is in perfect accord with his own avowal (p. 93) that the psychological unintelligibility of a dramatic character " shows only the incapacity or folly of the dramatist." We shall see that these expressions are in the present case unduly severe.

his characters, to account for their actions, to reconcile their inconsistencies, not as if they were the coinage of a human brain, but as if they had been actual existences upon earth. We talk of Hamlet the man, instead of Hamlet the *dramatis persona*—of Hamlet that God, in place of Hamlet that Shakespeare created. . . . It is not . . . the inconsistencies of the acting man which we have as a subject of discussion . . . but the whims and vacillations, the conflicting energies and indolences of the poet. It seems to us little less than a miracle that this obvious point should have been overlooked.[1]

Needless to say, it had not been universally overlooked, having been clearly put more than a century before Poe by Gildon and Hanmer, and again by Mackenzie; but when Hartley Coleridge said: " Let us, for a moment, put Shakespeare out of the question, and consider Hamlet as a real person, a recently deceased acquaintance," he was asking us to do what most of the later critics have commonly done, to the miscarriage of the problem. It is the course taken by Professor W. F. Trench in his commentary on the play, which only incidentally suggests possibilities of confusion in Shakespeare's work, and never at all contemplates the problem of adaptation of a previous play. This partly holds good, in fact, even of the admirable study of Professor Bradley, who so conclusively confutes alike the old subjective theory and the modern objective theory of Hamlet's procrastination, and so judicially, to my thinking, substitutes in effect, although he does not consistently adhere to, the explanation of psychic shock (if I may so phrase it) as being alone broadly compatible with the data. Hamlet, in short, as we see him, is neither weak of spirit nor really outmatched by mere circumstance. Even Werder falls back chronically on subjective solutions, as, for instance, that Hamlet feels at certain stages that he is not getting

[1] *Marginalia : Addenda* : Works, ed. Ingram, iv. 469–70.

help " from above "—a thesis as entirely gratuitous as
the formula that Rosencrantz and Guildenstern perish
partly because " they are not serving God." [1] This is
the theorist's way of discounting the fact that Hamlet
avows his own unjustified abstention from action.
Granting the theatrical view that there *has* been a surprising abstention, the candid course, though not the
final solution, is to say with Professor Bradley that something *in* or undergone by Hamlet withholds him from
the act of revenge ; and that this something is clearly
not mere over-reflection, even though Hamlet does talk of

> Some craven scruple
> Of thinking too precisely on the event,
> A thought which, quarter'd, hath but one part wisdom,
> And ever three parts coward.

The point is that after all his self-analysis he avows :

> *I do not know*
> Why yet I live to say ' This thing's to do ' ;
> Sith I have cause and *will* and *strength* and *means*
> To do't.

And the conclusion must apparently be, *if* we are to
frame a theory of " the man Hamlet " at all, that for
his soul, poisoned by the knowledge of his mother's guilt,
the act of vengeance is really no solace, fiercely as he
craves it from time to time. Life for him remains
poisoned, there being nothing that can fully revive his
will-to-live after that deadly injury. An adequate love-
motive is lacking, Ophelia being inadequacy incarnate.
For Hamlet, life is not worth living, and revenge is not

---

[1] *The Heart of Hamlet's Mystery*, trans. cited, p. 169.

worth taking save by way of final closing of the whole
account.

But this comparatively just though incomplete induction, to which the Germanic ethic of Werder made
him blind, is probably obscured for those who follow
him by reason simply of their habit of seeing HAMLET
as a planned play, not as a play of adaptation and
adjustment. We now know that such it was. Goethe's
account of the piece as something suddenly and wonderfully conceived by the poet [1] we now know to be a pure
chimera ; and Goethe would have confessed as much
if he had been told the play's history. And Professor
Bradley, who, if I read him aright, is at times in accord
with the construction above put, stops short, for the
same reason, of the verdict that HAMLET is not finally
an intelligible drama as it stands, though he nearly
pronounces it. That verdict we must face. Hanmer is
finally quite right : the poet *as dramatist*, having actually
put in Hamlet's mouth a repeated avowal of inexplicable
delay, should have given us a reason for it. And he does
not, precisely because his transmutation of the play was
but a process of making more and more mysterious a
delay which in the earlier story was not mysterious at all.
In the early story there *were* " objective " reasons for
Hamlet's delay, and these have been progressively elimin-
ated, leaving the harmonists to invent new. In the
early story Hamlet makes no self-accusals : these have
been expressly inserted, so that the harmonists are moved
to invent explanations. But explanations are just what
the dramatist has neither inserted nor indicated.

Those who argue that a reason is in any way *given*
are invariably found either to ignore or do violence to

[1] Eckermann, *Gespräche*, 1828, 11 März.

features of the play which conflict with their interpretation, or to impose upon it and us a thesis which the
whole play rejects. The latest experimenters conform
to the rule. Thus the Rev. Dr. H. Ford, in his SHAKE-
SPEARE'S HAMLET: A NEW THEORY (1900), claiming to
show " what was the poet's intention in the play," argues
that Hamlet's inhibition lies in his knowledge that
Christianity vetoed revenge.[1] Yet of such a conception
or motive there is not one hint in the entire play.   On
the contrary, not only does Hamlet many times vow
revenge and never once avow hesitation about its fitness :
he *takes* revenge on Rosencrantz and Guildenstern without a sign of subsequent remorse, whereupon Dr. Ford
declares that the deed " needs no apology. A justifiable
act of self-defence " [which it emphatically was not]
" carries with it no self-reproach." [2] And besides thus
substantially upsetting his own thesis, the theorist incidentally suggests that, " though conscience repels the
thought of revenge, Hamlet nevertheless uses conscience
as *a kind of subterfuge and excuse for not doing what he
has no intention of doing.*" [3] *Solvuntur tabulæ.* For the
rest, the critic also argues, as so many had done before
him, that Hamlet before his knowledge of the murder
is already shattered by his mother's incestuous marriage [4]
—all this by way of repelling the formula of " irresolution," which he mistakenly supposed to be so generally
held that his attempt to subvert it was a solitary protest.[5]
It might well survive his proposed amendment, which
is equally untenable, serving as it does merely to force

[1] Work cited, ch. ix.   [2] *Id.* p. 30.   [3] *Id.* p. 28.
[4] He quotes Furnivall (p. 62) as putting the strong proposition that
for Hamlet the murder of his father is " only a skin-deep stain " in comparison with his mother's guilt.
[5] *Id.* p. 5.

into new prominence the fact that the play cannot be explained *from within*.

A similar criticism is elicited by the more studious performance of Professor W. F. Trench, who, though he does not cite them, virtually adopts the formula of Schlegel and Coleridge and Lowell, accounting for Hamlet's non-performance by representing him as a man of contemplation, reacting only mentally, being from the first incapable of the required action.[1] The thesis seems unnecessarily complicated, not to say confused, by the further position that Hamlet is chronically " pretty mad " [2]—a theory which pretty well dispenses with the psychological analysis to which the writer devotes so much ability. The play is thus at once a " tragedy of inefficiency," [3] of " the will-less-ness proper to the contemplative genius," [4] and of a virtual insanity which is equally proper to that genius. We are therefore not to be surprised if we cannot understand Hamlet : " he cannot understand himself " [5]—a proposition surely no less applicable to half the characters in the play—or in any play. But at the same time " We find it hard, with Shakespeare's help, to understand Hamlet : even Shakespeare, perhaps, found it hard to understand him." Perhaps !

And when the critic, after denying that Hamlet can act, dismisses the slaying of Polonius with the remark [6] that " About this ' rash and bloody deed ' Hamlet is *insanely* unconcerned "—adding a footnote insisting that

---

[1] Work cited, pp. 74–9, 119, 137.
[2] Pp. 76, 86–7, 107, 131, 161, 163, 227.
[3] P. 172.   [4] P. 119, *note*.
[5] P. 143. On p. 138 we have : " It must be admitted that Hamlet did not *always* correctly analyse his own motives."
[6] P. 173.

his " I took thee for thy better " is only an afterthought —and again dismisses the doom of Rosencrantz and Guildenstern with the comment : [1] " A bloody thought *enabling him* to write a letter that will lead to their destruction," we seem entitled to doubt whether the critic understands Hamlet either ; whether, in fact, this whole business of " understanding Hamlet " is not a following of a will-o'-the-wisp, to be renounced in favour of the task of " understanding HAMLET." The light from within invariably resolving itself into a multiplicity of shifting lights, we are compelled to seek light from without.

§ 4. The Growth of the Play.

The history of the play is thus vital to the comprehension of it. A real life is the life of an organism ; and a biography, whether general or episodic, is a necessarily imperfect and selective presentment of a life by way of narrative, document, and explanation. Its final value is in proportion to the vividness and the consistency with which it presents the organic personality, whether that be consistent or inconsistent, *recognizing* the latter quality where it subsists. A fiction is a willed *mechanism*, simulating under an artistic form the presentment of the career of an organism ; and its artistic validity is finally in terms of its measure of simulative success. Now, though the author of a fiction may use the device of pretended doubt as to the motives of his characters by way of heightening illusion on one side, that device is proper only to the novel, which admits of commentary. A play does not ; and it is not rightly the business of

[1] P. 224.

a dramatist to leave a character unintelligible. In the words of Gildon, he is " master of the story " : that is, he ought to be. So obvious is this that when the failure happens we are entitled to infer either (*a*) oversight or confusion on the part of the dramatist, or (*b*) some difficulty imposed by his material.[1] And it is easy to show that, while Shakespeare is certainly capable of oversight and of occasional confusion, in this case he has suffered or accepted a compulsion imposed by material which, as a stage-manager revising a popular play of marked action, he did not care to reject.

In a word, the dramatist is conditioned on the one hand by his qualities, congenital and acquired, and on the other hand by his matter ; and when the matter emerges as a prior play, with striking situations which constitute its " drawing " power, the conditioning on that side is apt to be constringent. Professor Bradley sees and states with perfect clearness and fulness the probable play of the personal equation in Shakespeare, the effects or limitations of culture, pressure of time, fatigue over an uncongenial task, knowledge of the low standards and poor taste of the bulk of his audience, and so on.[2] But in HAMLET, the first of the great plays in which Shakespeare fully reveals his supremacy, there is far more evidence of superabundant power and of keen interest in the main theme than of haste or carelessness —apart from his habitual indifference to time measurement. When then the play falls short of intelligibility in itself, it is at once the economical and the necessary course to look for the solution in the conditions imposed

---

[1] Professor Bradley, who expressed himself more uncompromisingly (as cited above, p. 24, *note*) would presumably assent to this.

[2] *Shakespearean Tragedy*, 2nd ed. p. 75.

by the material. Without a study of these we are very much in the position of the geocentric astronomer, revolving in an incomplete induction. The history of the play alone elucidates the main issue.

II

THE DOCUMENTARY PROBLEM

§ 1. The Pre-Shakespearean Play.

MOST critics have long been agreed that there was a pre-Shakespearean HAMLET, PRINCE OF DENMARK—presumably that noted by Henslowe as played in 1594— and that its author was Thomas Kyd.[1] Nashe's allusions, in his address " To the Gentleman Students " prefaced to Greene's MENAPHON (1589), concerning " shifting companions that run through every art and thrive by none," leaving " the trade of *Noverint* whereto they were born " ; " whole *Hamlets*, I should say handfuls, of tragical speeches " ; " Seneca let blood line by line and page by page," " the Kid in Æsop " ; " Italian translations," and " twopenny pamphlets," point clearly and solely to Thomas Kyd. He was the son of a scrivener ; he is known to have issued at least one pamphlet, which is preserved, and to have translated Tasso's treatise on household management (1588), and he echoes Seneca throughout his SPANISH TRAGEDY. The earlier theory that " trade of *Noverint* " pointed to Shakespeare is ruled out alike by date and by biographical fact. The identi-

[1] The hypothesis was first put by Malone.

fication of Kyd, definitely begun by English writers,[1] has been carried further by Herr Gregor Sarrazin in his THOMAS KYD UND SEIN KREIS (Berlin, 1892), where actual survivals of Kyd's phraseology in HAMLET, especially in the First Quarto, are specified :

Bellimperia.	Farewell, my lord,
	Be mindful of my love and of your word.
Andrea.	'Tis fixed upon my heart.
	First Part of Jeronymo : Dodsley's Old Plays, 2nd ed., iii. 70.[2]
Leartes.	Farewell, Ophelia, and remember well what I have said to you.
Ophelia.	It is already lock't within my heart.
	Hamlet, 1st Q. Rep., 1860, p. 16.

Fair locks, resembling Phœbus' radiant beams,
Smooth forehead, like the table of high Jove.
Soliman and Perseda, 333.
Hyperion's curls ; the front of Jove himself.
Hamlet, Fol. III, iv. 56.

Importing health and wealth of Soliman.
S. and P. V, i. 24.
Importing Denmark's health and England's too.
Hamlet, V. ii.

Isabella.	O where's the author of this *endless woe ?*
Hieronimo.	To know the author were some ease of grief,
	For in *revenge* my *heart* would find *relief.*
	Spanish Tragedy, II. v. 39.
	Revenge it is must yield my *heart relief,*
	For *woe begets woe,* and grief hangs on grief.
	Hamlet, 1st Q. Rep. cited, p. 83.

---

[1] *E.g.* W. H. Widgery, *Harness Prize Essays on the First Quarto,* 1880, p. 100 sq. One of Sarrazin's parallels, given below, is indicated by Widgery, p. 160.

[2] This play is not Kyd's, but founded on his *Comedy of Don Horatio.* See below, p. 53 sq.

Bellimperia. Hieronimo, I will *consent, conceal,*
            And aught that may effect for thine avail,
            Join with thee to revenge Horatio's death.
Hieronimo. On, then ; and *whatsoever I devise,*
            Let me entreat you, grace my practices.
                        S.T. IV. i. 45 (V. 146).
Gertrude.   I will *consent, conceal,* and do my best,
            What stratagem *soe'er thou shalt devise.*
                        Hamlet, 1st Q. Rep. cited, p. 65.

The parallels to " Hyperion's curls " and " Importing
health " may be challenged on the ground that the First
Quarto does not yield them ; but as regards the last two
there can be no rebuttal. The Quarto lines disappear
in the Second Quarto and the Folio ; and they are plainly
Kyd's. Further, though the First Quarto certainly
consists mainly of Shakespeare matter, some of it greatly
mangled, some not, it has many passages which are
plainly non-Shakespearean. Professor Dowden, adhering
to a position taken up in the past by various . critics,
including Grant White and the German Mommsen, committed himself to the declaration :

For my own part, repeated perusals have satisfied me that
Shakespeare's hand can be discerned throughout the whole of
the truncated and travestied play of 1603. . . . With the exception
of the following lines :
            Look you now, here is your husband,
            With a face like Vulcan,
            A look fit for a murder and a rape,
            A dull dead hanging look, and a hell-bred eye
            To affright children and amaze the world,
I see nothing that looks pre-Shakespearean, and I see much that
is entirely unlike the work of Kyd.[1]

But the first and last propositions are beside the case,
since no one denies that there is a great deal of Shake-

---

[1] Introd. to *Hamlet* in " Arden " ed., p. xviii.

speare in the Quarto ; and the other denial was surely
an oversight. The " revenge " lines and the " consent,
conceal " lines, just cited, and seen by the Professor in
Sarrazin, *are* pre-Shakespearean ; and in a dozen places
we have a plainly pre-Shakespearean basis for passages
which Shakespeare rewrote. Take Ophelia's reply to
Laertes :

> Brother, to this I have lent attentive ear,
> And doubt not but to keep my honour firm ;
> But, my dear brother, do not you,
> Like to a cunning sophister,
> Teach me the path and ready way to heaven,
> While you, forgetting what is said to me,
> Yourself, like to a careless libertine,
> Doth give his heart, his appetite at full,
> And little recks how that his honour dies.

This is not a misreporting of the speech given us in the
Second Quarto : it is a transcript, probably imperfect
in two lines, of a speech in a feebler and flatter style and
versification. Similarly Ophelia's account to her father
of Hamlet's distraction begins in the First Quarto in a
non-Shakespearean style :

> O young Prince Hamlet, the only flower of Denmark,
> He is bereft of all the wealth he had ;
> The jewel that adorn'd his features most
> Is filcht and stol'n away ; his wit's bereft him ;

as does the speech of Polonius to the king and queen,
telling how he had ordered Ophelia to refuse the Prince's
addresses. It is earlier and poorer matter,[1] which in

---

[1] Mr. Widgery, in his brilliant prize essay (*Harness Prize Essays*, 1880),
finds Shakespearean quality in these passages. I cannot. Professor
Herford (essay in same vol., p. 84) partly leans to Mr. Widgery at this
point, but notes non-Shakespearean matter.

the Second Quarto is rewritten. The version of the
" To be " soliloquy in the first may possibly be only a
mangling of what we have in the second ; but this cannot
be said of the king's soliloquy in the prayer scene :

> O that this wet that falls upon my face
> Would wash the crime clear from my conscience !
> When I look up to heaven, I see my trespass ;
> The earth doth still cry out upon my fact,
> [Pay me ?] the murder of a brother and a king ;
> And the adulterous fault I have committed :
> O these are sins that are unpardonable.
> Why, say thy sins were blacker than is jet,
> Yet may contrition make them white as snow.
> Aye, but still to persever in a sin
> Is an act 'gainst the universal power.
> Most wretched man, stoop, bend thee to thy prayer ;
> Ask grace of heaven to keep thee from despair.

This is not a first draft by Shakespeare, any more than
it is a misreport of the soliloquy of the Second Quarto :
it is pre-Shakespearean. And these and other equally
non-Shakespearean passages are printed by Professor
Dowden in an Appendix, with no suggestion there that
they are unlike the manner of Kyd. They are in fact
quite in the manner of THE SPANISH TRAGEDY and ARDEN
OF FEVERSHAM.[1]

But we have further the phraseological clues given by
Widgery and Sarrazin, to which may be added these :

1. In the scene between Horatio and the Queen after
Hamlet's return, which appears only in the First Quarto,
we have the line :

> For murderous minds are always jealous,

---

[1] Kyd's authorship of *Arden*, first contended for by Fleay, and sup-
ported by the present writer in *Did Shakespeare write ' Titus Andronicus ' ?*
has been independently and conclusively established by Mr. Charles
Crawford (*Collectanea*, vol. i).

where *jealous* must be read as a trisyllable, *jelious*. The word is so scanned in the SPANISH TRAGEDY (II. ii. 56), and its occurrence with that scansion four times in ARDEN is one of the many clues to Kyd's authorship of that play. All four lines chime exactly with that cited.

2. The revenge-grief couplet quoted by Sarrazin from the First Quarto follows a line which also is an echo of Kyd, by himself :

> Therefore I will not *drown thee* in *my tears.*

Compare :

> To *drown thee* with an ocean of *my tears.*
> Spanish Tragedy, II. v. 23.

3. " As raging as the sea," in the Queen's speech to the King after the closet scene, is but a slight clue (*S.T.* IV. iii. 101) ; but in the line :

> He might be once tasked *for to try your cunning,*

in the First Quarto's version of the King's talk to Leartes after learning of Hamlet's return—a piece of dialogue clearly pre-Shakespearean—the " for to " points to Kyd, who uses that idiom eight times in ARDEN. The " for to " in the line :

> For to adorn a king and guild his crown,

in the First Quarto's closet scene, is probably a misprint for " fit to."

4. But there emerges here a further clue, noted by Professor Boas,[1] which clinches the other.   In the SPANISH TRAGEDY Bellimperia says (IV. i. 178) :

> You mean to *try my cunning*, then, Hieronimo.

These small coincidences become progressively significant as they accumulate ; and Professor Boas has noted yet others.

5. After the King in the First Quarto has remarked to Leartes : " He might be once tasked for to try your cunning," Leartes asks :

> And how for this ?

and the King begins his reply :

> Marry, Leartes, thus.

Exactly in the same fashion, in the TRAGEDY, when Hieronimo has been talking to Lorenzo of tragedy-writing, the latter asks (IV. i. 74) :

> And how for that ?

and Hieronimo replies :

> Marry, my good Lord, thus.

And in both cases the explanation given is met in the same way, Leartes saying, " 'Tis excellent," and Lorenzo, " O excellent."

---

[1] Introd. to Kyd's works, 1901, p. li.

6. Yet again, there is a close parallel of phrase and situation between the feigned reconciliation of Leartes and Hamlet in the First Quarto and that of Castile's son and Hieronimo in the TRAGEDY (III. xiv. 154). The King says to Gertrude :

> We'll have Leartes and our son
> Make friends and lovers as befits them both.

Castile says :

> But here, before Prince Balthazar and me,
> Embrace each other, and be perfect friends.

In both cases, as Professor Boas points out, the formal reconciliation is the prelude to the catastrophe.

7. Another echo noted by Professor Boas and others occurs in connection with the play scenes. Hamlet in the First Quarto (III. ii.) cries :

> And if the King like not the tragedy,
> Why then, belike, he likes it not, perdy.

So Hieronimo in the TRAGEDY (IV. i. 196–7) :

> And if the world like not this Tragedy,
> Hard is the hap of old Hieronimo.

8. And yet again we have the cry of Hamlet :

> I never gave you cause,

echoed in that of Lorenzo (*S.T.*, III. xiv. 148) :

> Hieronimo, I never gave you cause.

To refuse to see in this string of verbal coincidences a proof of the survival of portions of Kyd's original text in HAMLET is to evade phenomena which can be explained in no other way. They set up the same problem as we are faced-by in the multitude of echoes from Peele in TITUS ANDRONICUS. If we are to suppose Shakespeare in these cases composing a play of his own, we conceive him as parroting in the weakest way two of his contemporaries who were incomparably his inferiors in literary power. A tag or a poetic trope he might and did echo from other poets, as they so constantly echoed each other ; but here we have many phrases which are not current tags, and tropes not worth repeating. If Shakespeare penned them he was simply copying other men's humdrum dialogue, as if for lack of power to make his own independently. The conception only needs to be put clearly in order to be rejected. The young Shakespeare was not more but less likely than other men to plagiarize thus weakly and slothfully. In KING JOHN, as later in LEAR, he rewrites a whole play without copying a line.

Seeing, then, that in the parts of our play under notice there is no question of the intervention of any other hand, we are bound in candour and in common-sense, having regard to all the other cogent evidence for Kyd's origination of HAMLET, to decide that the score of echoes above noted signify the survival of so much of his matter in Shakespeare's first adaptation. In the relatively small quantity of clearly non-Shakespearean work detachable from the First Quarto, the number of the echoes is conclusive.

§ 2. The Old German Version.

But the really important problem is not so much to detach survivals of Kyd's phraseology in HAMLET as to ascertain with some precision what is of his determination in the structure and action of the play. We know from the early allusions that his Hamlet played the madman and cried " Revenge," and that the old play had a Ghost. So much might have been inferred from a comparison of the machinery in the existing play and the SPANISH TRAGEDY; and we might confidently infer that Kyd had introduced the play-within-the-play, and also the Dumb Show. As confidently might we expect him to delay the revenge of Hamlet in some such fashion as he delays that of Hieronimo; and to effect a similarly comprehensive catastrophe. Even the suicide of Ophelia duplicates that of Isabella.

But actions having a general resemblance might be handled very differently in detail, and to ascertain as closely as may be Kyd's actual procedure we must examine the old German play DER BESTRAFTE BRUDER-MORD, otherwise TRAGEDY OF HAMLET, PRINCE OF DENMARK, probably identical with the tragedy of " Hamlet, Prince of Denmark " known to have been played, with many other Elizabethan pieces, at the Court of Dresden in 1626.[1] This, though preserved only through a manuscript of 1710, is at bottom clearly an early form of our HAMLET.[2] Like the First Quarto, it has the name Corambis (Corambus in the German

---

[1] Cohn, *Shakespeare in Germany*, 1865, p. cxv. sq.

[2] Latham, in his *Two Dissertations* (1872) suggested that the German play may have been the original, and that the English travelling players may have brought the account of it home with them. This will not old for an instant.

play) for Polonius; and though the dialogue is visibly much retrenched, it apparently represents an earlier state of the play than that version. It possesses also a Prologue in which Night is the principal speaker, assisted by Alecto, Mægera and Tisiphone—in all probability a rendering of a prologue by Kyd.[1] Professor Dowden, demurring to the use of this play by Mr. John Corbin as evidence for his thesis[2] that the early Hamlet and Ophelia were turned to partly comic purpose, and that Hamlet was substantially a man of action, puts it as "far more probable that the German play is a debased adaptation of Shakespeare's HAMLET in its earliest form."[3] But that thesis really does not exclude that which it repugns, seeing that Dowden accepted Kyd's authorship of the 1589 HAMLET, and does not suggest that Shakespeare's is a wholly new construction. Granting as he does the origination, it is difficult to see why he should have doubted that the simpler conception of the hero seen in the German play points back to Kyd. It seems probable indeed that the primitive episode in which the German Hamlet contrives that the two ruffians commissioned to kill him (in place of Rosencrantz and Guildenstern) shall shoot each other when they mean to shoot him, is a substitution for Hamlet's narrative of the altered letter, which could not be staged. The story of the altered letter is in Belleforest's tale of Amleth, and so lay to Kyd's hand. But not only is the prologue markedly in the taste of Kyd's Ghost and Revenge epilogues in the SPANISH TRAGEDY and those of Love, Fortune and Death in SOLIMAN; the simpler action

---

[1] Cp. Widgery. as cited, p. 105. This is the answer to Latham's point that the German prologue suggests a German poet of some power.

[2] *The Elizabethan Hamlet*, 1895.   [3] Introd. cited, p. xiv.

of Hamlet is precisely what we should expect from him.

By Dowden's admission, there was a Ghost in the Kyd play : it is testified to in Lodge's allusion in WITS MISERIE in 1596 ; and there was a play-within-the-play in that piece as in the SPANISH TRAGEDY. The play-within-the-play in the First Quarto differs in diction and in character-names from that in the Second ; and is clearly primitive.[1] What kind of action, then, and what kind of psychology, was Kyd likely to put in his piece ? We should expect from him a delayed revenge, as in the TRAGEDY, but a revenge delayed simply—or partly—through lack of opportunity or fear of miscarriage, as in that case. Now, in the BRUDERMORD, Hamlet tells Horatio immediately after the Ghost scene what he has learned, and explains that he proposes to feign madness. That Hamlet *had* so enlightened Horatio is indicated in our HAMLET (III. ii. 81) as in the First Quarto, though the scene of the communication has disappeared in the process of transmutation which creates the mystery of the play. There is no hint of the kind of difficulty formulated by Klein and Werder—the impossibility of proving the king's guilt by citing the statement of the Ghost. Hamlet in the German play makes use of the visit of the players as in our play, but he writes nothing for them : he simply commands them to play the play of " King Pyrrhus," whose brother pours juice of hebenon in his ears as in our drama. The German Hamlet, like the English, is quite satisfied with the result, and he shows no paralysing melancholy. He is, in short, as much a man of action as Jeronymo, delaying only because

---

[1] On p. 180 of his Prize Essay, Mr. Widgery seems to assign the idea to Shakespeare ; but on p. 204 he admits that it was in the " Ur-Hamlet."

he must, though the delay is as it were artistically elaborated.

Before the advent of the players he explains to Horatio (II. v.) :

> By this pretended madness I hope to find opportunity to avenge my father's death. But you know my father [1] [*i.e.* the present King] *is always surrounded by many guards,* so that I may chance to miscarry, and you may find my dead body. Let it then be honourably buried, for on the first opportunity I find I will try to kill him.

Then, when Horatio suggests that the Ghost may be a deceiver, the actors arrive ; and although Hamlet has no doubts, he sets his trap by their means. It is all in Kyd's way of episodically developing and prolonging an action.

Equally simple has been Hamlet's action towards Ophelia, in which there is neither passion nor pathos. With her, he plays the pseudo-madman comically, not tragically, and his " get thee to a nunnery " is a ribaldry. All the same, his method in his madness arouses the suspicions of the King, as in our play, only Corambus and Ophelia being deluded, as in that. After the play scene, as in our tragedy, Hamlet has the chance to kill the praying King, and abstains, for the theological reason, with this noteworthy difference, that he bethinks him that to kill the praying person is to " take his sins upon thee." Then he goes to the Queen, seeking an audience, not sent for, and proceeds to reproach her, making reference to the pictures, as in our play. Corambus is hidden, as there, and is killed in the same fashion ; whereupon

---

[1] In the First Quarto, Hamlet twice addresses the King as " father." Rep. cited, pp. 50, 68 (at III. ii. 100, and IV. iii. 32). The word disappears in Q. 2 and Folio.

immediately the Ghost appears, with thunder and lightning, invisible and inaudible to the Queen. Hamlet
takes the visitation simply as a demand for the hastening
of his vengeance : there is no dialogue, and no real self-
reproach, any more than there is any sense of real guilt
on the part of Jeronymo when Bellimperia denounces
his delay. The delay in each case is for Kyd simply
the necessary involution of the drama. There is no
intentional mystery about his Hamlet.

Laertes (Leonhardus) in the German version returns
to avenge his father, and is pacified by the King, as in
our play : the main action is all given. The King, however, plans the poisoned foil as in the First Quarto,
Laertes doubtfully assenting. There is no burial of
Ophelia. She has gone mad, in a fashion to entertain
the groundlings. Here, perhaps, there has been a German
vulgarization, for Kyd had the tragic sense ; but the
German Phantasmo, to whom the mad Ophelia attaches
herself, reveals the basis of Osric. Hamlet has paid no
further heed to Ophelia ; and when at the outset of the
fencing scene the Queen brings the news of her suicide,
the fencing goes on without a pause ! Here again there
has probably been compression.

At the beginning of the fifth Act Hamlet is simply
concerned because his vengeance is still delayed, the
fratricide being " always surrounded by so many people."
" But I swear," he adds, " that ere the sun has made
his journey from the East to the West, I will revenge
myself on him." Then he tells Horatio of his experiences
(there is no graveyard scene), and is interrupted by the
arrival of Phantasmo with the invitation to the fencing
match. Hamlet fools with Phantasmo in the fashion
in which in our play he fools with Polonius ; but immedi-

ately afterwards is struck with apprehension and faints with terror because his nose bleeds. He accordingly goes to Court with a foreboding, and the fencing takes place as in our play, with the difference that the news of Ophelia's suicide is interjected as aforesaid, at the outset.

The changing of the foils, the wounding and confession of Leonhardus, the King's proffer of the poisoned drink, the Queen's interception of it, her death, and Hamlet's stabbing of the King, all follow in due course. But there is no glad acceptance of death on the part of Hamlet, who tells Horatio that his soul is now at peace, seeing that he is revenged ; and that he hopes his wound will amount to nothing. In his lament for his mother, who has " half earned this death through her sins," he inquires who gave her the poisoned drink, and, learning that it was Phantasmo, stabs him. Then the poison o'ercrows his spirit, and with his dying breath he tells Horatio to carry the crown to Norway to " my cousin, Duke Fortempras, so that the kingdom may not fall into other hands. Oh, alas, I die." And Horatio winds up with a brief discourse, ending with four lines of sententious verse. There has been no previous mention of Fortempras, which again is doubtless a result of curtailment, as the entire German play is not half the length of the SPANISH TRAGEDY.

And here we are led to face a problem that seems to have been ignored by all save one hostile critic of HAMLET, that, namely, of the superfluous matter in the structure as it stands. The German play has the distinction of eliminating a quantity of detail that in no way helps the central action, reducing that to comparative simplicity and unity. There is thus a presumption that the existing version is the result of successive compressions. HAMLET is the longest of all the Shakespeare plays, having 3,931 lines to the 3,332 of the long LEAR ; yet the BRUDERMORD is the shortest of the three principal German versions of Shakespeare tragedies reproduced by Cohn—considerably shorter than the TITUS ANDRONICUS, and much shorter than the ROMEO AND JULIET. There is, in fact, more removable matter in HAMLET than in any other of the plays named. How then came it to be present ?

KYD'S PROBABLE CONSTRUCTION

§ 1. Superfluous Survivals.

So many admiring critics have pronounced HAMLET a gravely faulty play that it is unnecessary to labour the general proposition. Seldom, however, has the verdict been accompanied by a careful analysis; and that is now our business.

In 1873 the German poet Benedix, in his work DIE SHAKSPEREOMANIE, carrying on the debate on that theme which began in Germany with the tercentenary of 1864, contended that HAMLET is ill-constructed in respect of five episodes which have only the effect of hampering the action :

(1) The despatch and return of the embassy to Norway have not the slightest interest for us. But weeks or months [1] must pass before the embassy returns.

(2 and 3) The journey of Laertes to Paris, and the sending of Reynaldo after him, are equally irrelevant. The directions of Polonius to Reynaldo have no interest for us, and we are left waiting for his return, which cannot take place for weeks or months.

(4) The journey of Fortinbras through Denmark to

---

[1] This seems excessive. A few weeks would suffice.

Poland, involving the use of ships, must take months, and for his return also we are kept waiting.

(5) Hamlet's journey to England puts off the dénoûment just when the action is heightening, and leaves us again waiting.

> "We thus see," sums up Benedix, "four persons travel away out of the piece ; and not till late do they come back again. These journeys are wholly superfluous episodes. They cause the time of the action to be extended many months ; and it is due to these episodes, and to them alone, that Hamlet's slowness becomes such a mystery. The fourth Act looks like an interpolation introduced in the previous play." [1]

If we take up the position which seems implicit in Professor Bradley's method of interpretation, that Shake-speare's *use* of the prior material is to be considered his *plan*, such criticism as the above, in so far as it may be valid, tells for us not only against the play but against the playwright ; and it is a pity that Professor Dowden should have thought fit to dismiss the criticism of Benedix as merely trivial.[2] It is not trivial ; and if Shakespeare is to be justified in the traditional manner it must be faced.[3] Even if it be claimed that Hamlet's dismissal to England is part of the original saga, and is rightly to be embodied as part of his " weird," there arises the demurrer that the playwright has altered the saga by arresting Hamlet's voyage and bringing him back, thus merely lengthening the action without any effect on the sequel. As for the episodes of the embassies, the mission of Reynaldo, and the campaign of Fortinbras, they are

---

[1] Furness's Variorum *Hamlet*, ii. 351.

[2] *Shakspere Primer*, p. 165.

[3] Professor Trench in his " Commentary " (p. 49) not only says nothing of the irrelevance of the embassy in Act I. sc. ii., he comments : " And now to business."

visibly excrescences on the plot as they stand, seeing
that even the impression made by the expedition on
Hamlet, rousing him to a fresh vow of immediate action,
does not produce such action, the dismissal to England
supervening all the same.

But that the fourth Act was framed as a whole by
Shakespeare merely to make out the five is a weak and
false hypothesis. The play is far too long for stage
purposes ; the first Act could easily have been divided
into two at the fourth scene, where we have a new and
important action ; [1] and the fourth Act contains the
necessary plot for the fencing scene. It was, moreover,
certainly given in the main to Shakespeare by his original.

As regards the embassy, the mission of Reynaldo, and
the expedition of Fortinbras, the case is different. These
are in no way necessary, as the play stands, to the final
action ; and, for that very reason, to suppose that
Shakespeare invented them is to impute to him a kind
of gratuitous mismanagement impossible to him as a
practical playwright. Rather we must assume that they
too were given him ; and pronounce that his error lay
in retaining them. The Reynaldo scene is either a
retention of a previous scene that is practically super-
seded by the actual introduction of Laertes, or an attempt
at a *genre* effect such as we find so often in Chapman
and Jonson. The disappearance from the German play
of all the scenes named is a result of the recognition of
their superfluity either by the original English actors
who took the play to Germany or by some later German
adapters.

---

[1] See below, p. 56, as to the cessation of the numbering of Acts and
scenes in the Folio after II. ii. It is generally agreed that Act IV has
been wrongly divided, its earlier scenes belonging to Act III.

That the episodes of the embassy and the expedition were given by Kyd is the hypothesis forced upon us by a study of the structure of the play in comparison with that of the SPANISH TRAGEDY. That the mission of Reynaldo was given by Kyd is more doubtful, though we have it in the First Quarto, with the name Montano instead of Reynaldo. If it be not Kyd's, it is still presumably pre-Shakespearean : that is to say, it is highly unlikely that Shakespeare was the first to load the play with such an irrelevance as it finally amounts to. But it is just possible that in an earlier form of the play Reynaldo's mission counted for something in the action, even as there is reason to think that the embassy and the expedition of Fortinbras had a part in an original action still more multifarious than the present.

An obvious objection to such a suggestion is that for any more widespread action there was simply no room, unless we suppose that much of the dialogue in the existing play was wholly unrepresented in the original. But I do not propose to employ this rebuttal : there is an alternative explanation.

§ 2. Was Kyd's "Hamlet" a Double Play?

Over twenty years ago I tentatively put forward the hypothesis that HAMLET as we have it may be a condensation of a double play. The suggestion, so far as I know, met with no discussion ; and I have not till now repeated it ; but to-day, on a fresh survey of the problem, it still seems to me a possible solution of the evaded problem. Three circumstances should be noted before it is discussed on its merits :

1. About the time of the publication of HAMLET,

Shakespeare was concerned in the reduction of Whetstone's two-part play of PROMOS AND CASSANDRA to a single play, MEASURE FOR MEASURE.

2. There were current a number of sequel-plays;[1] and there is strong reason for thinking, with Fleay, that JULIUS CÆSAR as it stands is a compression of two plays into one.

3. Kyd's SPANISH TRAGEDY is a member of a double play. Henslowe enters a *Spanes* (*Spanish*) *comodye donne oracoe* in February 1592, and this is repeatedly played on a day before *Jeronymo*—the old name for the SPANISH TRAGEDY.

It cannot have been the existing FIRST PART OF JERONIMO, printed in 1605. The old COMEDY was probably not new in 1592. It is the fourth play named in the Diary, which at this point appears to continue a previous record, now lost. Written before 1592, it could not have had such a number of double endings as the existing FIRST PART, which has forty-four in the first Act, as against only a dozen in the whole TRAGEDY. The FIRST PART being further in the main markedly different in style from Kyd's work, Mr. Greg and Professor Boas agree that it is much later (*circa* 1600 ?), adding that it is not a comedy.[2] As to this I would make a demur. The original play must, like this, have included the death of Don Andrea, by way of preluding the TRAGEDY, yet it was called a comedy; and there are many instances in which serious drama was in those

---

[1] On the French stage of the period, sequences sometimes ran for as many as eight days—an outcome of the old practice in " mystery-plays." The fullest extension of sequence on the Tudor stage occurred in the case of the Chronicle plays, which would give the cue to sequels in general drama. Chapman has thus two double-plays in the next decade.

[2] *Henslowe's Diary*, ed. Greg, ii. 150.

days styled " comical." [1]   Deaths did not necessarily
make a tragedy, provided that the hero was successful,
and Horatio is so in the FIRST PART. That play, then,
is presumably a rewriting of the old COMEDY OF DON
HORATIO, preserving its main action, and probably parts
of its text ; and we are left with the presumption that
Kyd wrote the COMEDY, whether before or after JERONIMO
it is impossible to guess.

On the whole it seems to have been much less successful than the TRAGEDY, for while we have in Henslowe
several sequences of " doneoracio " and " Jeronymo,"
the latter is far more frequently played by itself throughout 1592. It was played by Lord Strange's men, and
does not appear in the repertory of the Earl of Sussex's
company in 1593–4, or in those of the combinations of
the Queen's men and Sussex's, or the Admiral's men
and the Lord Chamberlain's, in the same years. Not
till 1597 does JERONYMO reappear [2] in the Diary ; and
the COMEDY never reappears at all, while the other goes
on steadily.

Assuming that the FIRST PART proceeds on the main
lines of the COMEDY, and that the COMEDY was Kyd's,
we may get some light from the former on Kyd's mode
of construction. It starts with an embassy from Spain
to Portugal to demand over-due tribute. A refusal
leads to the fighting in which Don Andrea is killed. Don

---

[1] E.g. The Comical History of Alphonsus King of Arragon, by Greene,
printed in 1599.

[2] Creizenach (Gesch. des neueren Dramas, IV. i. 539) notes that " Jeronymo " is entered in Henslowe's Diary on 7th January, 1597, as " ne "
(new), and, taking the reference to be to the First Part, pronounces that
the priority of the Tragedy [now generally admitted] is thus proved.
But the reference is probably to a mere reproduction of the Tragedy
with some new matter. " Ne " frequently means this in Henslowe.
If it were the First Part he would have called it so. " Jeronymo " is
always his name for the Tragedy.

Balthazar, the Portuguese Prince, is hot for refusal, and fights valiantly. He is primarily a counterpart of Fortinbras ; and there is ground for a presumption that Kyd would have given the latter more than a merely negative part to play. The " post-haste and romage in the land " described in the first scene of HAMLET is dramatically irrelevant to the present action ; and the story of the combat between the fathers of Fortinbras and Hamlet ultimately serves no purpose save to prepare for the succession of Fortinbras at the catastrophe. Was it introduced solely for that purpose ? Kyd's method, in the light of his practice, would have been to send the ambassadors to Norway at the outset ; and it is quite conceivable that the King's speech at the outset of Scene ii, which we find in the BRUDERMORD beginning almost exactly as it does in our play, but *without* the item of the embassy, was originally the beginning of the piece, *with* that item. It would in fact be properly so placed, chronologically ; for the marriage has taken place before the Ghost appears. There has clearly been a rearrangement of scenes and speeches even as between the First and Second Quartos ; and the " To be " soliloquy is left ill-placed. It would come properly before the Ghost scene, speaking as it does of " the bourne from which no traveller returns." [1]

The obvious effectiveness of the Ghost scene as an introduction would explain easily its transference to that position, supposing it to have been originally placed later. Kyd's method indeed would presumably have

---

[1] It is even conceivable that this speech, in a pre-Shakespearean form, was originally written for another play. It has no proper place in *Hamlet* after the Ghost scene. It might have held the place of the present soliloquy in I. ii.: " O that this too, too solid flesh would melt " ; but that, too, in a prior form, is in the First Quarto.

been to prelude with a Ghost prologue ; and to develop that into a dramatic scene would be in the obvious course of theatrical development. As it is, the preparations of Fortinbras are idly made to explain " this our watch," as if there would not be sentinels on the King's castle at all times. Such rearrangements of play-openings take place on our own stage in the case of non-literary pieces. It is to be observed, too, that the scene in which Hamlet sees the Ghost is not numbered in the Folio, and that after the second scene of Act II the numbering of Acts and scenes ceases altogether. Apparently there has been a rearrangement which upset the original divisions.[1] As the case stands, Hamlet's scene with the Ghost, which takes much longer to play than to read, would make an Act in itself.

One possible clue to the original employment of the Fortinbras motive is given in the German play, in the scene in which, before meeting the Ghost, Hamlet tells Horatio how the King has had himself crowned while Hamlet was in Germany ; " *but with a show of right he has made over to me the crown of Norway,* and appealed to the election of the States." It seems impossible to account for this passage as a German invention, since it in no way concerns the remaining action. It must surely belong to the pre-Shakespearean play. And the presumption is that on this pretext Kyd brought his Hamlet and Fortinbras into some conflict, which not only filled the stage for a time but prepared for the bequest of the crown at the close.

As it is, the account of the old combat between the

---

[1] As there is great diversity throughout the Folio as to the numbering of Acts and scenes, it cannot be specially argued from in the case of *Hamlet* ; but probable rearrangements would seem to be the likely explanation in most of the cases.

kings of Denmark and Norway presents a situation in which the lands of the elder Fortinbras—that is to say, the Kingdom of Norway [1]—had been forfeited to the elder Hamlet, King of Denmark. Such a situation would provide an action lengthening the play to such an extent that the death of Polonius, followed by the dispatch of Hamlet to England, may have been the conclusion of a " First Part," leaving the second to begin with the return of Laertes to seek *his* revenge. And such a break would give the necessary interval for the return of Laertes, which is now lacking.

Such a procedure seems likely enough for Kyd. Duplication seems to have been the note of his early work. In the Kyd HAMLET, a " murdered Ghost " figures as in the TRAGEDY ; a play-within-a-play figures in both ; Fortinbras, as aforesaid, pairs with Balthazar ; Laertes seeks to revenge his father as does Hamlet, merely inverting the order of the TRAGEDY, where the father revenges his son ; Isabella's madness and suicide are duplicated in Ophelia's ; and the suicide of Ophelia in the German play resembles that of Jeronymo. Beginning the second play with the Laertes motive, Kyd might carry on the two themes side by side with the Norwegian complication and the madness of Ophelia.

§ 3. Irrelevant Scenes.

But it would not be in Kyd's way to introduce Laertes without letting us see him informed of his father's death ; and that consideration brings us to the conundrum of the mission of Reynaldo-Montano, which clearly derives

---

[1] In the old Hamblet story, the combatants are originally not kings but pirate chiefs. Hamblet's father marries the king's daughter.

somehow from a pre-Shakespearean source. That Shakespeare invented such a purposeless episode as the present merely to exhibit the character of Polonius is unthinkable. On the other hand, the scene is not at all in the manner of Kyd. As it stands, it suggests the intervention of another hand between Kyd and Shakespeare, though Shakespeare may have revised.

Such irrelevant scene-writing is the specialty of Chapman, alike in comedy and tragedy. It is abundantly exhibited in MONSIEUR D'OLIVE, where the subsidiary character o'ercrows the plot; and it appears to be Chapman's hand that developed Parolles in ALL'S WELL.[1] As our play now stands, the only conceivable motive for the Reynaldo scene is the theatrical need for comic relief after the tremendous Ghost scene. But if we suppose the mission of Montano-Reynaldo in the original play to have served a purpose in the action, we may guess that in that Montano played the part of a messenger to Laertes with the news of his father's death. On that view we might doubtfully guess that Corambis had been dispatching him on the eve of the play-scene, and that the news of the death, following immediately afterwards and before Montano's departure, replaced the proposed mission. But this is highly problematic; and we can but insist on the obvious probability that the existing scene is neither by Kyd nor by Shakespeare, save in so far as Shakespeare may have recast it.[2] If Kyd had an equivalent scene, it may have stood at the beginning of Act III.

A similar problem arises as to the " To be " soliloquy.

---

[1] See *Shakespeare and Chapman*, pp. 264, 270, 272.
[2] There are twelve double-endings in the first nineteen lines—a *very* high proportion for Shakespeare.

That, as it stands, obviously clashes with the fact of the appearance of the Ghost ; and it is difficult to believe that Kyd had the idea of making Hamlet contemplate suicide immediately after vowing to revenge his father —unless, indeed, by way of crudely shamming madness ; or in a state of partial despair at non - success, like Jeronymo.

In the German play, there is no hint of such a mood ; and in the place where it would have been appropriate in our play—the first Act, *before* the revelation of the Ghost—the ground is already covered by the soliloquy which follows the dialogue of Hamlet with the King and Queen. In the First Quarto, the soliloquy—which here, albeit the text is corrupt, indicates a somewhat different form—follows on Corambis' account to the King and Queen of Hamlet's love-melancholy upon Ophelia's rejection of his suit. The Queen withdraws, and the King listens to the soliloquy and the subsequent dialogue with Ophelia ; the " fishmonger " talk following. In the Second Quarto, as in the Folio, Polonius entreats the King and Queen to go, proposing *another* opportunity for their overhearing such a dialogue ; and we have at once Hamlet's " fishmonger " dialogue with him, fol-lowed by the entrance and dialogue of Guildenstern and Rosencrantz, and the advent of the players ; the " To be " soliloquy and its sequel being relegated to the third Act. All this rearrangement cannot have been the work of the piratical editor. It tells of a protracted process of reconstruction.

It is an open question, then, whether the " To be " soliloquy is an early item in Shakespeare's transmutation of Hamlet into a pessimist ; or whether an original speech has been removed by him, recast, from a more appro-

priate place ; or whether it was originated by the hand
or hands that had begun to recast the play before he
took it up. As it stands, the versification appears to
be his in the first form as well as in the second, allowance
being made for the reporter's corruptions.

For the rest, while we may certainly ascribe a play-
within-the-play to Kyd, with some dialogue on the
functions of the players as we have it in the BRUDERMORD,[1]
it is tolerably certain that neither the player's Pyrrhus-
speech nor the existing interlude is by him. The fact
that Hamlet in the German play begins by recalling a
" Pyr-Pyr-something," and that a king Pyrrhus is there
the counterpart of the Albertus of the First Quarto and
the Gonzago of the Second, raises speculation ; but
the player's speech and the interlude as they stand are
not Kyd's. I have elsewhere suggested that both may
be the work of Chapman, and that Hamlet's compli-
mentary account of the play from which the Pyrrhus
speech was taken may thus have been a tribute to the
" rival poet " from Shakespeare. There is the alternative hypothesis [2] that, as it is certainly an imitation
of Marlowe's DIDO, the imitation may have been made
by Shakespeare in order to pay a compliment to Marlowe,
perhaps after his death. But the existing play-scene I
take to be Chapman's work.[3] The absolute echo of
Greene in the opening lines raises the question whether
that poet may here have collaborated with Kyd in the
original play, or added something to it later, as he seems
to have done to some extent in ARDEN. But if so,
Shakespeare or another had ejected Greene's work to

---

[1] Admittedly parts of the advice to the player in Q. 1 are non-
Shakespearean.

[2] Put by Widgery, as cited, p. 161.

[3] See *Shakespeare and Chapman*, p. 215 sq.

begin with, for the version in the First Quarto differs entirely at the outset from that in the Second, the Greene lines being absent. The solution I would offer is that the interlude as it stands in the First Quarto is substantially Kyd's; that Chapman may have inserted the passage with the line (echoed in his WIDOW'S TEARS):

> None weds the second but she kills the first,

which is a duplication of the thought in the Queen's next lines; and that he later rewrote the scene for the company, echoing Greene's lines after he had revised Greene in ALL'S WELL, where there is a similar passage.[1] I do not agree with Mr. Widgery that the opening lines in the First Quarto version are beyond the power of Kyd: they seem to me quite possible to the Kyd who translated CORNELIA; and they are really not good enough for Shakespeare.

Kyd it certainly was that introduced the madness and suicide of Ophelia, perhaps vulgarizing the madness in part as is done in the BRUDERMORD in the episode with Phantasmo. But it is his hand that gives the King's lines:

> Ah, pretty wretch, this is a change indeed:
> O June, how swiftly runs our joys away!
> Content on earth was never certain bred;
> To-day we laugh and live, to-morrow dead.

These cannot be Shakespeare's. Neither did Shakespeare write the scene between Hamlet and his mother as it stands in the First Quarto. Even Professor Dowden

---

[1] See *Shakespeare and Chapman*, p. 266. In *Selimus*, which is certainly in the main Greene's, there is yet another use (l. 41) of the formula there sampled.

gave up part; and the remaining lines wholly lack Shakespeare's touch, though their versification is regular. As we have seen, they include a duplication of lines in the SPANISH TRAGEDY. The lines are probably Kyd's down to the end of the scene.

As for the next, in which Fortinbras passes with his troops, it is probable that Hamlet's soliloquy, Second Quarto, which alone motives it, was already written when the First Quarto was issued, but was dropped in the representation as it is dropped in the Folio, for sheer lack of time. But to Kyd, finally, must we attribute the scene, lacking in the Second Quarto, in which Horatio tells the Queen of Hamlet's safe return—an episode which here is very slightly handled, Hamlet having been simply " set ashore " after having altered the King's letter so as to doom the two courtiers. The scene may have been curtailed; but it is certainly non-Shakespearean, and the line :

But murderous minds are always jealous (jelious),

with its peculiar scansion, points definitely to him. The opening speech by Horatio is probably a rewriting of an earlier; it has four double-endings in seven lines, which Kyd would not have produced in 1589; but the writing is not Shakespeare's. The rest is in Kyd's early manner. Whether he had a graveyard scene it is impossible to guess; but Ben Jonson's phrase, " sporting Kyd," suggests that he did some humourous work; and in the rest of his preserved matter we have none save the Basilisco scenes in SOLIMAN AND PERSEDA, scenes which cannot quite confidently be assigned to him. He may then have introduced a graveyard scene by way of carrying on Hamlet's pretence of madness, which never amounts to much in his hands, so far as the writing goes in the First Quarto and the BRUDERMORD. The probability is that his Hamlet, like the Hamblet of the story, indulged in mad action, to eke out a pretence that was inadequate in respect of the dialogue.

One thing should here be incidentally noted. The association of Horatio with the Queen at the first entrance of Ophelia, in the Second Quarto, is probably due to the simple fact that, Polonius being dead and the missioners gone, there is no other known courtier to introduce. But the arrangement works ill; for Horatio thus knows of Ophelia's madness, yet tells Hamlet nothing of it before the funeral scene. There was no careful reconstruction here.

IV

SHAKESPEARE'S WORK OF TRANSMUTATION

§ 1. Old Action: New Psychosis.

It remains to note how Shakespeare's handling has turned a Hamlet who was very little of a mystery into a Hamlet who is very much one. The first step in counter-sense, certainly, was taken by Kyd, when he combined the revelation by the Ghost with the mock-madness of the old story given him in Belleforest. In that, no Ghost is needed, the murder being known to all, though the traitorous brother (Fengon) persuades the people that he killed Hamblet's father (Horvendile) only in defence of Geruth, Hamblet's mother, who is secretly Fengon's paramour. Hamblet's madness, accordingly, is assumed in the manner of the old myth of Brutus and David, to save his life, he feeling sure that otherwise Fengon will slay him. It is not primarily a matter of wild talk but of demented action, though Hamblet proceeds to make " subtill answers " which arouse Fengon's suspicion, leading him to seek to entrap the youth by means of a " fair and beautiful woman " and " certain courtiers." Here we have the germs of Ophelia and Rosencrantz and Guildenstern ; and in the foster-brother who puts Hamblet on his guard we have a hint of Horatio.

Another attempt is made by Fengon to entrap Hamblet in a talk with his mother, with a counsellor concealed behind the hangings,[1] and the counsellor is killed by Hamblet in the manner of the play, which here also follows the story. Before the slaying scene, however, Kyd had previously composed the play-within-the-play, which gratuitously reveals to the King Hamlet's ghost-given knowledge of the murder—a fresh confusion of the old plot. In that, the killing of the courtier is followed by Hamblet's dispatch to England; his counterfeiting of the letters, so as to doom the messengers, as in the play; and his manifold English adventures, which the play ignores.

Whereas, then, the barbaric Hamblet shams madness to save his life, Kyd's Hamlet, who shams madness after supernaturally learning of a wholly secret murder, thereby begins at once to endanger his. Apprised by the Ghost, he had no occasion to alter his behaviour: it was his business to behave as before, the King having thus far no designs on him. And the play-within-the-play is another supererogation. Kyd loved to complicate his motives thus. In ARDEN he introduces items of sacrilege and avarice which are dramatically needless, being motived only by the academic principle that he who suffers must have sinned; and he invents two wronged men, one of whom appears merely to curse, doing nothing further in the action. By thus confusing the original Hamlet-plot through his favourite Ghost-motive, Kyd, led to retain the mock-madness by his success with the semi-madness of Jeronymo, prepared the divagation

[1] Under straw in Saxo Grammaticus; under a quilt in Belleforest. The hangings appear in the English translation, of which only a copy dated 1608 exists.

which Shakespeare so wonderfully develops. The Ghost-warned Hamlet who shams madness to no purpose grows naturally into the Hamlet who unintelligibly swerves from revenge.

That Kyd's inconsistencies of construction thus inhere in Shakespeare's play is a fact which criticism must sooner or later face. Lowell, rightly arguing that "if you deprive Hamlet of reason there is no truly tragic motive left," confuses his position by accepting the absurd pronouncement of early Victorian "experts" that Hamlet really exhibits in perfection the symptoms of madness, and explains that "if such a man assumed madness, he would play his part perfectly." Then he remembers that the assumed madness is "one of the few points in which Shakespeare keeps close to the old story," and accordingly declares him to have done so with "unerring judgment." Hamlet, that is to say, shams madness merely because he does not know what else to do: "the scheme of simulated insanity is precisely the one he would have been likely to hit upon, because it enabled him to follow his own bent, and to drift with an apparent purpose," and so forth. Then we are to believe that Shakespeare saw in the expedient of the barbarian of the story, a man of action absolutely, "precisely" what would be done by a man of exactly opposite structure. To such shifts does idolatry conduct us.

We shall ultimately do much more for Shakespeare's credit by honestly acknowledging that his Hamlet pretends madness because Kyd's Hamlet did so before; and that in Kyd's Hamlet the device is put out of joint, first by Kyd's own further device of the Ghost's revelation, which cancels the prudential motive of the saga

Hamblet, making Hamlet on the contrary at once arouse the King's suspicion ; and secondly by the device of the play-within-the-play, which is anything but a madman's plan, though Jeronymo gave the precedent. In a word, Hamlet's mock-madness is now ill-motived. Lowell, in his best " high priori " manner, writes that " Voltaire complains that he [Hamlet] goes mad without any suffi- cient object or result. Perfectly true, and precisely what was most natural for him to do, and, accordingly, precisely what Shakespeare meant that he should do." What Voltaire really said [1] was that " pour ne pas donner d'ombrages à Gertrude, il contrefait le fou pendant toute la pièce "—a jest which incidentally suggests a better motive for Hamlet's mock-madness than any given by the idolaters. As criticism, Voltaire's fling is perfectly just ; and, like some of his other flings it is to be met, not by brazening things out, but by granting that Shake- speare did at times make himself answerable for other men's artistic sins.[2] He did so when, essaying his immortal task of transmuting the crude play of Kyd into a dramatic marvel, he retained all the archaic machinery while transfiguring all the characters. A marvel his *tour de force* remains ; but no jugglery can do away with the fact that the construction is incoherent, and the hero perforce an enigma, the snare of idolatrous criticism.

It is of no avail to plead, as Mr. Widgery so eloquently does after Werder, that Hamlet in the play has an in- superably difficult task, seeing that he cannot prove the King's guilt by citing the testimony of a ghost. Why

[1] *Lettre à messieurs de l'académie française,* 15 auguste, 1776.
[2] *E.g.* the scene between Henry and Catherine in *Henry V*, which Voltaire contemned. Most of his attacks on Shakespeare turn on real blemishes, and they are bracketed with very high praise. The sin of his criticism is its want of final balance.

did he not at the outset tell both Horatio and Marcellus what the Ghost had told him? They would have believed, and been believed, readily enough. Given a Ghost who is credited by the *audience*, why should he not be credited by the characters? When, again, the King rushes away in confusion from the play, it is surely idle to argue, as does Mr. Widgery, that Hamlet has failed in his object because the King does not *speak*. Is not his confusion a sufficient proof of his guilt? To say that the courtiers do not so recognize it is to argue in a circle. Shakespeare would never have *planned* a play on such lines and with such a thesis, any more than he would have invented the prayer-scene and the motive that there withholds Hamlet.

All these devices, once more, are but the machinery of Kyd, adapting a barbaric story in which the barbarian *must* delay his revenge because he is only one against a powerful chief, whom the people heartily support, believing him to have saved the youth's mother from her husband's violence. It all goes back, possibly, to a sun myth; but the barbaric tale is fairly coherent. Kyd needed a tale of delayed vengeance, and for him, though he makes Hamlet indirectly accuse himself in the closet-scene with the Ghost,[1] there was no more mystery in Hamlet's delay than there was in Jeronymo's, or in the halting and hindered movement of the action in ARDEN, with the baffled attempts, and the two reconciliations of the doomed man with his enemy. Kyd's tragedy-method was not psychological or didactic, with all his devotion to Seneca: it is one of protracted and long-

---

[1] In Q. 1 the dialogue is clearly in part Kyd's; and in the *Brudermord* we have the same deprecation of the supposed wrath of the Ghost at delay.

baffled action; and he of necessity ekes out the time with incidents and expedients, especially where, as in HAMLET, he has a plot full of delays given to his hand.

In the closet-scene in the First Quarto, the Ghost says nothing of an " almost blunted purpose "; that is Shakespeare's modification. Kyd has no such conception. His Hamlet says:

> Do you not come your tardy son to chide,
> That I thus long have let revenge slip by ?

but the Ghost replies only :

> Hamlet, I once again appear to thee
> To put thee in remembrance of my death.
> Do not neglect, nor long time put it off,—

going on to urge him to comfort his mother. This is wholly in the spirit of the SPANISH TRAGEDY, where the partly unavoidable and partly artificial delay of revenge is the great preoccupation of the distracted Jeronymo, who delays in order to obtain a grand finale of slaughter by means of his play-within-the-play. He begins plotting immediately after the murder :

> Meanwhile, good Isabella, cease thy plaints,
> Or at the least dissemble them awhile :
> So shall we sooner find the practice out.
>
> II. v. 113.

When he gets Bellimperia's letter he is suspicious :

> Hieronimo, beware,—thou art betrayed.
> And to entrap thy life this train is laid.
> Advise thee, therefore, be not credulous. . .
> Dear was the life of my beloved son,

> And of his death behoves me be reveng'd :
> Then hazard not thine own, Hieronimo,
> But live t' effect thy resolution.
> I therefore will by circumstances try
> What I can gather to confirm this writ. . . .
>
> III. ii. 37–49.

He contemplates suicide and refrains :

> For if I hang or kill myself, let's know
> Who will revenge Horatio's murther then ?

He thinks of appealing to the King, but decides to " go by, go by." He

> will revenge his [Horatio's] death,
> But how ? not as the vulgar wits of men,
> With open but inevitable ills,
> As by a secret yet a certain mean,
> Which under friendship will be cloakèd best.
> Wise men will take their opportunity
> Closely and safely, fitting things to time ;
> But in extremes advantage hath no time ;
> And therefore all times fit not for revenge.
> Thus therefore will I rest me in unrest,
> Dissembling quiet in inquietness—
>
> III. xiii.

and so on. Revenge, awaked from sleep by Andrea's ghost (an item which has been mistakenly ridiculed), replies :

> Sufficeth thee that poor Hieronimo
> Cannot forget his son Horatio,
> Nor dies Revenge although he sleep awhile.
>
> III. xii.

Bellimperia bitterly reproaches Hieronimo for his delay, but he reassures her and plots on ; Isabella, committing suicide, denounces his negligence ; but he is all the while at work. For Kyd, Hamlet was substantially in the same case ; and in making the prince excuse himself to the Ghost he is not implying that Hamlet has been really remiss. That is Shakespeare's development of the situation. Professor Bradley subtly argues[1] that when the Ghost says " Remember me " he is touching, not accidentally, on a faculty of forgetting known to him in Hamlet ; but in all probability the touch came from Kyd. When Jeronymo says (III. vi. 103) :

> This makes me to *remember thee*, my son,

he does not mean that he had ever forgotten him.

§ 2. The Infusion of Pessimism.

The vital dramatic difference, however, between Jeronymo and Hamlet was that while the audience saw and followed Jeronymo's purpose, there was no very clear purpose in Kyd's Hamlet to follow. The question, put to this day by the unsophisticated, " Why doesn't he kill his uncle and live happy ever afterwards with Ophelia ? " was forestalled by Kyd only in so far as he offered the explanation given in the BRUDERMORD, that the King is always surrounded by his guards. That explanation, given him in the old story, probably seemed to him sufficient. But he in effect partly qualified it when, multiplying his episodes after his manner, he staged the play-scene, which put the King on his guard, and then the prayer-scene. If meantime, as we have surmised, there had been going on an action in connection

---

[1] *Shakespearean Tragedy*, p. 126.

with Fortinbras, Elizabethan audiences would be apt to be impatient.

True, once more, there has been no great delay in all : indeed, save for the indefinite interval between Acts I and II there has been none at all! The play-scene is only a day after the arrival of the players ; and on that night the action rushes on to the point of the decreeing of Hamlet's voyage to England. After being convinced by the King's behaviour, Hamlet has had but one chance to slay him ; and to stress that one recoil as the critics do is to pay a remarkable tribute to the " time-devouring " power of Shakespeare's dramatization. Hamlet, when all is said, is commonly condemned on the strength of a single recoil from assassination, and that under circumstances in which, religion apart, any high-minded man would have recoiled. To stab the King in the back while he knelt praying would have been truly a precious proof of " resolution " and " faculty for action." But the fact remains that, as Shakespeare's added soliloquies imply, the audiences, disregarding, under the dramatic spell, all questions of real time, fidgeted, without the modern critics to help them. They would have scouted the suggestion that a ghost was not a good witness ; after the convincing play-scene they would grow suspicious ; and after the prayer-scene many must have been moved to sarcasm, though doubtless Kyd's edifying theology impressed some. The broad fact is that, time apart, Hamlet as it were wilfully delays in our play, while Jeronymo is constantly planning his comprehensive vengeance, and loses no clear opportunity, though he too is slow, to the extent of angering his wife and Bellimperia.

Now, Shakespeare's handling of the play is above all

things a masterly effort to hint a psychological solution of the acted mystery, while actually heightening it by the self-accusing soliloquies. It is he who makes Hamlet keep the Ghost's tale secret : in the BRUDERMORD it is at once revealed to Horatio ; and in our play we learn at the play-scene that it *had* been revealed in the interim. It is he who stresses the Queen's guilt, here reverting to the original story as against the treatment indicated in the BRUDERMORD, where the King makes no charge against his wife, though Hamlet speaks doubtfully of her at the close. In the First Quarto we have the Ghost's speech on the battlements from the text given in the Second ; but in the closet-scene the Queen protests her absolute ignorance of the murder, and pledges herself, in lines that are obviously Kyd's, to assist Hamlet against the King. Here Kyd follows the Belleforest story, in which Geruth protests her innocence of the murder, saying nothing of other matters. In the Second Quarto these passages disappear, and though Hamlet does not accuse the Queen of complicity in the murder, his tone is that of one who has suffered tortures on the score of his mother's degradation.

This, if there be any, is the new ground note of Shakespeare's Hamlet. The guilt of a mother is an almost intolerable motive for drama, but it had to be maintained and emphasized to supply a psychological solution, or rather a hint of one. The childlike subserviency of poor Ophelia tells to the same effect.[1] Utter sickness of heart, revealing itself in pessimism, is again and again dramatically obtruded as if to set us feeling that for a heart so crushed revenge *is no remedy*.[2] And this implicit

[1] Professor Bradley's gallant and brilliant defence of the ill-starred child does not alter her relation to the action.

[2] Never that it is forbidden by religion.

pessimism is Shakespeare's personal contribution: his
verdict on the situation set out by the play.[1] But the
fact remains that he has not merely not been explicit—
as he could not be—he has left standing matter which
conflicts with the solution of pessimism; he has exhibited
Hamlet as roused to determination by the spectacle of
the march of Fortinbras and declaring that he knows
not why he has refrained; and he has further exhibited
him acting with abundant vigour in the sea episode, as
he had previously done in planning the Court play. These
displays of vigour, like the killing of Polonius, do not
consist with a pessimism so laming as to preclude revenge.
And the ultimate fact is that Shakespeare *could not* make
a psychologically or otherwise consistent play out of
a plot which retained a strictly barbaric action while
the hero was transformed into a supersubtle Elizabethan.

§ 3. The Upshot.

If this be pronounced aspersive criticism, I have but
to say that for me the play becomes only more wonderful

[1] Over thirty years ago I put the thesis of Hamlet's pessimism in an
essay on *The Upshot of Hamlet* (1885). It has since been independently
put by several German writers, who however leave the issue at that.
See Hermann Türck's *Hamlet ein Genie*, 1888, and *Das psychologische
Problem in der Hamlet-Tragödie*, 1890; also his polemic with Kuno
Fischer over their respective originalities: *Die Uebereinstimmung von
Kuno Fischer's und Hermann Türck's Hamlet-Erklärung*, 1894; and
Kuno Fischer's kritische Methode, 1894. Both writers, as it happened,
were repeating a British thesis. But Türck has the phrase: " Hamlet
is the tragedy of idealism " (*Hamlet ein Genie*, p. 17), partly endorsed
by Professor Bradley, p. 113. On the other hand, my proposition that
Shakespeare imports a temporary pessimism of his own into Hamlet's
situation was partly anticipated by Rümelin in his *Shakespearestudien*,
1866, p. 96: " So war auch in Shakespeare die Hamlet-natur nur ein
Theil seines Gemüthslebens." But he again was anticipated a century
earlier by a British critic who far outwent his age in psychological pene-
tration: " For what is Falstaff, what Lear, what Hamlet or Othello,
but different modifications of Shakespeare's thought ? "—Maurice
Morgann, *Essay on Falstaff*, 1777, p. 16.

when the manner of its evolution is realized. What Shakespeare could not do, no man could have done. What he did remains a miracle of dramatic imagination. In the place of one of the early and crude creations of Kyd, vigorous without verisimilitude,[1] outside of refined sympathy, he has projected a personality which from the first line sets all our sympathies in a quick vibration, and so holds our minds and hearts that even the hero's cruelties cannot alienate them. The triumph is achieved by sheer intensity of presentment, absolute lifelikeness of utterance, a thrilling and convincing rightness of phrase, and of feeling where wrong feeling is not part of the irremovable material. He who will may argue that Shakespeare should not have accepted intractable material. Let him tell us whether he would rather have been without HAMLET, and whether he cannot see that the practical compulsion to handle or retain intractable material underlies half a dozen of the Shakespeare plays as well as HAMLET,—TIMON, PERICLES, CYMBELINE, HENRY V, the WINTER'S TALE, MEASURE FOR MEASURE, ALL'S WELL, to say nothing of other comedies. Till that is seen, Shakespeare is not revealed.

He was, as usual, adapting an old play for his company, in the way of business. Its main features he had to preserve, else the public would miss what they looked for. HAMLET must retain its Ghost and its mock-madness, no less than the real madness of Ophelia. To satisfy the poet as well as his cultured patrons, the Prince must be made truly princely ; and every stroke to that end was an element of success. But the revenge of the refined

---

[1] This, of course, does not apply to *Arden*, which is later, and psychologically very much superior to the *Tragedy*, though little better in point of verse technique.

Hamlet must be delayed as was that of the barbaric Hamblet, without the original reason ; the old machinery must be retained, down to the prayer-scene ; and so there emerged a puzzling and unexplained character in place of one analogous to the rudely and clearly outlined Jeronymo, never puzzling to anybody save the characters alongside him, who are not in his counsels as the audience are.

Evolving a Hamlet of the highest mental lucidity, Shakespeare himself at one point accepted the inference of an " almost blunted purpose," a will that will not act when it should ; and by a score of subtle strokes he tacitly suggests how a man may feel the barrenness of a revenge to which he is vowed. • But this is only half of his composite Hamlet : the other is the presentment of a man who can act with lightning speed and force, and will " make a ghost of him that lets me." Of all the explanatory formulas, that of Mackenzie, so little discussed, is the best.[1] He posits an excess of sensibility which yields uncertain and divergent action—a spirit which recoils as uncontrollably from straightforward killing as from another's villany or unworthiness. With a difference, Professor Bradley pronounces that Hamlet " tries to find reasons for his delay in pursuing a design which excites his aversion."[2] Such a conception may as easily be read into Shakespeare as that of psychic shock, or pessimism arising out of personal disillusionment. But it also is inadequate to the data. Hamlet thrusts through the arras without hesitation, and shows no horror at his deed. He has no scruple about sending

[1] The essay on *Hamlet* is not included in the collected edition of Mackenzie's *Miscellaneous Works*, 3 vols. 1820.

[2] *Shakespearean Tragedy*, p 226.

his schoolfellows to their death on the bare surmise that
they knew the contents of the King's dispatch. A " sensibility " which yields at once these results and an insuperable recoil from vengeance on a villain is not finally
thinkable. In the words of Salvini, " A man like Hamlet
has never existed, nor could exist."[1] This, as we must
admit in the conclusion, is not really an ultimate indictment of Shakespeare : but it is a necessary estoppel of
certain theorists who turn an æsthetic suggestion into
a false historic theorem.

When, on the other hand, we can see so clearly how
Shakespeare was artistically committed to a series of
barbaric actions which had nothing to do with either
sensibility or pessimism, but which he had yet to assign
to a prince in whom sensibility and pessimism were
artistically developed by himself for the very purpose
of dramatic verisimilitude, it is idle to follow the dogged
defensive tactics of Werder, who was determined to find
a consistent whole where such does not exist.

The whole of Werder's polemic, as we saw, is a defiance
of the two vital soliloquies (II. end ; IV. iv.) in which
Hamlet impeaches himself. To call these, as Werder
does, " protests against the circumstances," is to do
sheer violence to the text. Hebler was able to confute
the thesis on the sole basis of the first,[2] convicting Werder
of grotesque misconstructions—partly due, it may be,
to the translation he followed.[3] But Hebler's own
solution was only less unsatisfying. Insisting on the
subjective solution, he formulated a " defective com-

---

[1] Art. " Salvini on Shakespeare," by Helen Zimmern, *Gentleman's
Magazine*, February 1884.

[2] Art. *Die Hamletfrage*, in *Im neuen Reich*, 1875, No. 41.

[3] Cp. *The Heart of Hamlet's Mystery*, note by translator, p. 44.

mingling of blood and judgment," [1] resulting not in a defect of will but in a defect of efficiency—" not a Will-not but a Can-not," " grounded in his [Hamlet's] personality." [2] This formula in turn merely evades the many instances in which Hamlet *can* act with instant and decisive force ; and we are left with nothing better than the nugatory notion that a man cannot do what he does not do. The problem of the play is merely baulked : we get an argument in a circle.

The German battle-royal of the seventh and eighth decades of last century is in fact but a protracted process of thesis-seeking, in which every device is tried to explain the problem without looking to its genesis. Rümelin, who came nearest doing so, was biassed by his purpose of combating " Shakespeare-Mania " and convicting the idol of clay feet, or at least clay toes. Rightly turning back to the old saga for the starting-point, he wrongly reasoned that all the difference between that and the final play is of Shakespeare's making ; never inquiring how fresh foundations may have been laid in the intermediate play, though he actually refers [3] to the First Quarto, and might by comparing that with the BRUDER-MORD, in the light of the Kyd-hypothesis, have seen the necessity of reckoning with other determinants than the saga and Shakespeare. Rightly enough he pronounces the play to have been often retouched ; and he makes the very intelligent suggestion that the duplication of Hamlet's fooling with Polonius and Osric cannot have been original, but must have come of a readjustment, what was intended as a substitution of effects being by oversight allowed to result in a repetition. But he sees

[1] Art. cited, p. 562. [2] *Id.* p. 571.
[3] *Shakespearestudien*, 1866, p. 90.

nothing of the pre-Shakespearean construction, and so gets by a leap to the theory of " an unsatisfactory inter- weaving of an episodical, modern-subjective element in the old-northern saga " [1] (a theory which, he avows, will not untie all the knots), laying the whole procedure at Shakespeare's door.

Hebler countered Rümelin by a *tu quoque!* He summed up that in Rümelin's view Shakespeare sought (1) prim- arily and ostensibly to represent the saga-Hamlet and not a loiterer (*Saümer*) ; (2) but, as suited him best, at the same time a creature of his own spiritual cast ; and (3) was thus compelled to make him a loiterer, albeit one who reproached himself for being so. To which Hebler retorted that Rümelin himself had gone through the experience he ascribes to Shakespeare : that Rümelin began (1) with the saga-Hamlet, but found himself (2) caught by the idea of Shakespeare's introduction of his own personality into the matter ; and so was led to the third view—of Hamlet as a self-reproaching loiterer— by way of modifying positions first and second.[2] How- ever that may be, Rümelin ends in sheer arbitrariness when he pronounces that Shakespeare's Hamlet differs from the barbarian in that " he must end tragically, *like all the figures* in which the poet has poured perilous stuff (*Krankheitstoff*) out of his own mental life—like Werther, Clavigo, Faust, Eduard." [3] As we know, Shakespeare's Hamlet simply had to end tragically because the play was a tragedy to begin with.

All the while, Rümelin was at one point nearer the true line of criticism than Hebler, inasmuch as, in Hebler's words, he substituted a thesis of " Faults of

[1] *Id.* p. 87.   [2] *Aufsätze*, as cited, pp. 214-15.
[3] *Shakespearestudien*, p. 96.

the Poet" for that of "Faults of the Hero." It was much sounder than Werder's "Faults of the Situation"; and only needed revision and development to yield a "positive" critical method. But among them the German combatants reached no solid ground; and Rümelin, who became unfairly identified with the "Anti-Shakespeare-maniacs" who followed, is not even named by Max J. Wolff in his outline-list of German critical pronouncements on HAMLET.

That writer in turn, who ranks as the leading Shakespeare critic in latter-day Germany, carries the geocentric principle of interpretation to a height of fantastic complexity which it is to be hoped will be the signal for a resort, even in Germany, to positive methods.

Rejecting Goethe's formula as the most unfit of all, and ignoring Werder's, he combines a whole series of subjective solutions with a new one to the effect that Hamlet is the representative of *Truth* against a world of falsities, which at the same time he cancels by the added formula that Hamlet "*will not*" act. His exposition works out, in brief, thus:

1. "At one stroke the rôles of the tragedy are distributed" (in the "seems, madam," speech): "Here Hamlet as representative of Truth; on the other side the court, the world of show." Hamlet stands alone with Horatio and the despised players. "To them, the professional cultivators of show, Truth must take her flight, for all other *milieus* are closed to her." "After your death you were better have a bad epitaph than their ill report while you live";—*because* "*then* the comedians are the voice of Truth" (!).

2. Hamlet sets himself to be the reformer of the *time* —to put right the disjointed world.

3. " But this is not to be accomplished by man, or by Hamlet, but without him, or against him, only through the indwelling moral power of Truth."

3a. A God is needed to fulfil the mission.

4. A great tragic irony lies in the exposition. All human foresight is fruitless.

5. The Prince reacts to every new impression. [Mackenzie's formula, unconsciously adopted.]

6. He is a dilettant. [What else could a prince be ?]

7. Having had no discipline of duty, therefore, he is " himself an enigma," and therefore he refuses when for the first time duty enters his life with her behests.

1a. Yet the moral ideal within him makes him worthy to be the champion of Truth, however many human failings he may also have.

8. Pessimism, however, had already overwhelmed him.

9. So his uncle's crime does not appear to him as one man's guilt. All mankind is responsible for it.

9a. " His pessimism shuts out for him the knowledge that in the person of the crowned murderer he can and should tear up the root of the evil. He lets pass the moment indicated (*gewiesenen*) by Fate. [Which ?] . . . he neglects doing what he should and can, to hang on to it plans for world-betterment which overpass human powers." [Where does he so plan ?]

10. " Hamlet *will not* avenge his private wrong. As to this he is quite clear from the start." He shows it by the entry in his tables (!).[1]

8a. " This appeals to his mood, as consummating his

[1] This verdict is also given by Professor Trench.

pessimism, which under all outward show has scented corruption."

10a. " Because he *will not* act, because he *will not* undertake the plainly prescribed deed laid upon him, he will tell his friends nothing." [How then comes he to tell Horatio later ?]

10b. " Hamlet relates himself quite passively to his task. He *cannot* reform the world ; he *will not* punish his uncle." [1]

These, I think, are all the motives and explanations, put in their sequence. It seems impossible to put more " points in Hamlet's soul " : the geocentric method has been diligently exhausted. And it is all to no purpose. Formulas which are in conflict cannot be reduced to unity by imposing either a general formula of Truth-seeking which would equally apply to LEAR and OTHELLO, and is therefore neutral to all, or an arbitrary " will not " formula which is never given save by reducing to the form of an accusation the perplexity set up by the delay in the action. The delay was there from the start, as the dramatic datum of an original action in which there was no thought of Truth *versus* Show, or World-Betterment, or overruling Providence, or over-susceptibility, or pessimism, or the fatality of dilettantism in princes, or the refusal of the hero to act. The motive of the original story is to follow the hero's *way* of acting. This remains the motive of Kyd, who, however, by altering the basis fatally confuses the movement. Shakespeare, by immensely heightening the character, puts it in still further irrelation to the action, giving us one great satisfaction in forgoing another.

---

[1] *Shakespeare, der Dichter und sein Werk*, von Max J. Wolff, 3te Aufl, 1913, ii. 120–7.

It is true that he *indicates* over-sensibility, and a pessimism which makes action seem vain ; but he also presents other and contrary things, and he *could not* indicate a " will not " which would cancel all the rest of the play, or a " plan " of reforming the world which would explode it. He can be clearly seen inserting soliloquies which absolutely posit the *need* for an explanation. That at the end of the third Act is a self-impeachment by Hamlet which avows as much ; and it is clearly an addition made without close heed to what goes before ; for Hamlet talks of arranging for a play as if he had not already arranged one with the players—unless that previous arrangement is itself an addition which takes no note of the soliloquy.[1] So with the soliloquy at the passage of the army of Fortinbras, an expedient of the same kind, designed to satisfy or pacify the auditors who wanted to know why Hamlet did not commit the right murder instead of the wrong one. Of course it could not satisfy ; and, inserted as it is in the Second Quarto, we find it dropped from the Folio, evidently as having been dropped from the prompter's copies. Written

---

[1] Professor Trench confidently argues (pp. 109, 111, 122, 124, 160, 225, *note*) that after arranging to supply the players with a new speech for *The Murder of Gonzago* Hamlet " resolves to substitute for that an original play of his own composition." This will not stand. The play finally *is* " The Murder of Gonzago " (III. ii. 249, 273, 275) ; and Hamlet instructs the player to " speak *the speech* . . . as I pronounced it to you." In the First Quarto the players are " the Duke and Dutchesse," not " King and Queen " as in the Second and in the Folio. To say that in the actual play-scene he " changes the name of his *Mousetrap* to that of a play that was before his mind on the previous day " is quite unwarrantable ; the " name " is a jesting one spontaneously thrown out, not the real title of a new piece. Not that we are necessarily to suppose that there *was* such a play, though there may have been [Albertus is the Duke's name in Q. 1 : and " Lucianus, nephew to the King," seems to mean " to the King of Guyana," which there takes the place of " Vienna "] ; but that the thesis of Hamlet's inability to keep to any plan is gratuitous. The *dramatist* is the factor.

in Shakespeare's vividest verse, it does but aggravate the perplexity by assuming that Hamlet has much need to excuse himself, and avowing that he cannot. Instead of suggesting or sanctioning a theory of either subjective or objective hindrance, it negates both. It is almost as if the dramatist, anticipating Lowell and Professor Trench and the rest, were censuring his own adopted creature. But that, of course, is not Shakespeare's way. He has simply decided to accept inexplicable delay as the formula of a play which reached him with that character apparently stamped upon it.

For it is idle to pretend that Shakespeare was deeply concerned to secure perfect artistic consistency. As an adaptor and reconstructor he worked wonders; but he had to let pass many incongruities, in many plays. To those already noted we may add the retention of the Dumb Show, in which, before the play, the murder is enacted even as it is after the speeches. As it is the action and not the speaking that upsets the King, he ought either to have been upset by the Dumb Show or to have collected himself for the repetition.[1] Shakespeare at this point merely let stand what he found, as he let stand the episodes which we have seen to be " out of the frame." Whether or not by reason of the play being originally in two parts, it is full of fortuitous retardations; and it is not surprising that in a recent revival the actor-manager dropped such matters as the advice to the players and Polonius' advice to Laertes; even as the Reynaldo scene had been dropped long before.

It is possible, indeed, to exaggerate the incongruities of the piece. Though Hamlet's age is certainly a conundrum, Professor Bradley has perhaps made needless

[1] This was commented on a century ago

difficulty [1] as to Hamlet's proposed return to Wittenberg.
" Going *back* to school in Wittenberg " does not necessarily
mean that he has just come thence ; and his reception
of Horatio and Marcellus does not imply, as Professor
Bradley says, that he and Horatio are supposed to have
left Wittenberg " for Elsinore less than two months ago."
Hamlet may have left it years before ; and his " Horatio,
or I do forget myself," suggests long severance. As
Professor Trench remarks, " the city " may very well
be Copenhagen, where Hamlet may have spent time
after leaving Wittenberg. But there is real incongruity
in his telling Horatio (III. ii.) how he has prized him
" since my dear soul was mistress of her choice," after
greeting him with " Horatio—or I do forget myself."
Even Professor Trench, who assures us that Shakespeare
is " regular and orderly in his work with the regularity
and order of a classical genius," [2] and warns us that
when we fail to understand it may be our own fault,[3]
also declares [4] that " when we fail to understand him
[Shakespeare], it certainly is often his own fault."

It is most true, if we must say " fault " in a case, where
the master is performing a miracle of transmutation,
vitalizing, elevating and irradiating a crude creation into
a world's wonder, and finally missing artistic consistency
simply because consistency was absolutely excluded by
the material. He leaves it possible for some (including
Professor Trench) to think Hamlet more or less really
mad. He indicates no totally explanatory formula because
he could not : the play will not now go into any. In
paying ourselves with saving formulas of Hamlet's mystery we are but obscuring Shakespeare's mystery, which

[1] In Note B on *Hamlet* in *Shakespearean Tragedy*.
[2] P. 187.   [3] P. 166.   [4] P. 109.

is here finally so legible and so vividly interesting. HAMLET is only the more wonderful for being rightly " understood." When Furnivall indignantly rejected [1] the thesis of the Clarendon Press editors that the First Quarto in its construction is mainly the work of the earlier playwright, he was but revealing the uncritical temper of the older Shakespeare-worship. Disregarding the real tests of diction and psychology, he was staking Shakespeare's greatness on such positions as the invention of the idea of a play-within-the-play and the creation of such dialogue as Hamlet's " chaff " with Polonius—work within the capacity of lesser men than Kyd. The assailed editors had made a loyal induction from the documents ; and Furnivall and Dowden, refusing to make it, were seeking for Shakespeare the wrong kind of credit. His real triumph was to turn a crude play into the masterpiece which he has left us. It is a perfectly magnificent *tour de force*, and its ultimate æsthetic miscarriage is only the supreme illustration of the vulgar but ancient truth that an entirely satisfactory silken purse cannot be constructed, even by a Shakespeare, out of a sow's ear —if one can without indecency apply that figure to a barbaric saga which ultimately yielded us HAMLET.

Æsthetically, it is improper. For, when all is said, the " pragmatic " test is practically final for such a thing as a drama. HAMLET has " made good " : it has enormously overpassed the simple end of the playwright, to entertain. The miraculous puppetry of the actor-manager has kept millions at gaze for centuries now ; and if Shakespeare could be recreated and asked why he managed here and there so oddly, he might with an unanswerable effect open eyes of wonder and ask what should make

[1] *Academy*, August 7, 1880.

us thus put his mechanism to the rack. " Do you want an *absolute*," he might ask, " as a stage entertainment ? " And though we might make play with Hamlet's dictum about holding up a mirror to Nature, we should be met by the reminder that that too is part of the *play* ; and we should know that Shakespeare had non-suited us.

And so he might silence us if we sought to debate with him on the character of Iago, which in Professor Bradley's fine dissection we almost feel to be drawn from life itself. " Did you mean to make a study of moral insanity ? " we might ask him : " is the formula of Iago simply that he is at bottom *the* criminal type, crafty in will-worship and stupid in craft—a reversion to the ape or savage ? " " Does that really matter ? " he might reply. " Has not the play sufficed to *occupy* intelligent people ? What matters it whether Iago could or could not have really existed ? Could Othello ? Could Falstaff ? For that matter, could *any* imagined person ? What *is* fiction ? . . . The play works. Would anything but Iago serve to drive a tragedy that hinges on a handkerchief ? If you think so, try another." And there an end.

But the critical intellect too has its rights : *its* concern is simply conceptual truth ; and as against—*not* Shakespeare but—those who formulate Ptolemaic schemes of his works, its rights are absolute. The " purpose of playing is "—well, not exactly what Hamlet-Shakespeare alleges ! But the purpose of science is indisputably to know how things actually went ; and it is time we had done with Ptolemaic methods, though the literary Ptolemaists have included some remarkably able men, recalling the distinguished prototype, who was a very able man indeed.

INDEX

For Product Safety Concerns and Information please contact our EU
representative GPSR@taylorandfrancis.com
Taylor & Francis Verlag GmbH, Kaufingerstraße 24, 80331 München, Germany

9 781138 996120